To Wilda -

With great admiration
and affection

"Sr. Marie Timothy"

Nancy 2002

A Nun's Journey

Nancy Hogan

Associated Publishers
West Palm Beach, Florida 33401

Published 2002

FIRST EDITION

Cover and book design by Mel Abfier

Designed and produced by StarGroup International, Inc.
West Palm Beach, Florida 33401
Web site: www.stargroupinternational.com

Printed in the United States of America

Library of Congress Cataloging-in-Publication Data
Pending

A Nun's Journey - Nancy Hogan
ISBN 0-9643958-6-X

A Nun's Journey

Nancy Hogan

**ASSOCIATED
PUBLISHERS**

Dedication

To my mother, Mary, who gave me the gift of life, instilled religious and moral values in me at an early age, and encouraged thoughtfulness at all times. I attribute my success in life to her, and I am grateful for her and to her.

Table of Contents

Preface

I have wanted to write about my experiences in the convent ever since I left the order of the Sisters of Notre Dame de Namur some thirty years ago. Many friends along the way encouraged me to pursue the telling of my story and, as time elapsed, I felt more and more compelled to deliver my message in the spirit of St. Julie.

Though I've left the sisterhood, but the sisterhood has never left me. St. Julie's character and courage will always be with me. Her strength and spirit are intertwined with my soul.

That's why I decided it was important for me to share my life's story. My experience taught me that it was important for each of us to answer our calling. Each calling may come in a wide variety of forms. Not all of us are called to God's service, though we are all called to do God's will. He loves us and He has a purpose for each of us. We see this as a passion; He sees it as our mission. God intends for us to follow what's in our hearts, whether it's to become a nun, a priest, a teacher, a doctor, a nurse, a lawyer, a carpenter or a laborer. We just have to listen and respond. I know that God intercedes daily for us and that we are all specially loved. He will never abandon us.

I pray that my book will provide an inspirational awakening for those who feel abandoned, lonely and unloved. Just as St. Julie's message of accepting God's goodness moved and motivated me throughout my life, I wish to move and motivate others to recognize just how good the good God is.

My goal is to encourage you to keep your faith, and never give up hope, and to ensure you that, in so doing, love will prevail.

Acknowledgements

A *Nun's Journey* would not have come into being without the friendship of my many friends who encouraged and prodded me over the years. To Brenda Star and her team of specialists in the publishing world – and above all the commitment and skill of my writing partner Shawn McAllister – without whom this book would not have found its way to paper. I'm so thankful the Lord brought us together.

Nancy served the Lord in the convent for 21 years. She has had an interesting life, with varied roles. Her energy, charm, sense of commitment and responsibility prepared her well for the 20th century challenges.

Gregory H. Adamian
President Emeritus and Chancellor
Bentley College
Waltham, Massachusetts

Hope Springs Eternal

In his first letter to the Corinthians, Paul said the three most important things in life were faith, hope and love. My life can be explained definitively in those terms. They describe my blessings and pinpoint my greatest challenges.

I was born and raised a Roman Catholic. My faith has constantly been intact — so much so that it has guided most of my life-changing decisions.

Love was always a driving force in my childhood, not because there was an abundance of it, but because I felt a shortage of it. I'm sure my parents loved me. They just didn't demonstrate it. They were not a physically demonstrative couple and never hugged each other or me. By most standards, I had it pretty good. I was showered with material things — clothes from Aunt Nell, bikes from Aunt Eliza, money from Nana and Grandpa — and never lacked for much, except to be hugged. My parents lost a child shortly before I was born, so I suppose their reservoir of expressive love had run dry.

In any case, I was raised in a very strict environment that had little room for displays of affection. My mother, especially, subjected me to stringent disciplines. In fact, all the adults in my youth seemed to have too many other things to worry about than showing any kind of affection for me, causing me to search for love from a very early age. In my search, I eventually began to distinguish my love for God separate from the love of others, which sometimes caused me anguish.

But I never lost hope. However, hope is often fleeting and not easy to hang onto. That, probably more than anything else, has been my journey — seeking, finding, understanding, accepting, and manifesting the most elusive aspiration of all — hope.

That challenge, combined with the age-old conflict between devotion to God and the temptations of humanity, best describes my character. I was born to be a nun. My task was to discover why.

I suppose you can say it started on the day of my birth, April 26, 1934, in Beverly Farms, Massachusetts. Beverly Farms is a small, illustrious community on the North Shore of Boston notable as the homestead of such eminent families as the Cabots, Lodges, and Freichs, and that conspicuously liberal and judicially poetic Supreme Court Justice, Oliver Wendell Holmes, Jr. I came to learn years later that "The Great Dissenter," as he was known because of his often-boisterous disagreements with the views of his colleagues on the Court, had a close connection to my father. My father was Timothy O'Brien, who for many years served as the famed justice's chauffeur.

The weather around Boston in April is always chilly and predictable as spring becomes determined to replace winter. That frequently results in meteorological turmoil that can be downright intolerable. It seems appropriate that I would arrive under such conditions.

My mother was the former Mary Healy, the daughter of Irish immigrants. I called her Mum.

"It's a girl!" Mum continually announced from her bed at Beverly Hospital in the days following my delivery. I suppose that was meant to be a comforting thought to my father, but there was little consoling him in those days. They had buried my sister just five months earlier.

Both Mum and Dad grieved deeply over the loss of little three-year-old Mary Ann to the croup. I can only imagine how they must have suffered trying to endure the torture of caring for their ailing infant daughter as she struggled through respiratory difficulties and incessant coughing. They could do little more than watch her ache until she suddenly died.

Dad blamed Mum for Mary Ann's death. The doctors told them that nothing could be done about her cough. They tried to continue their life as normal as possible. One night they went to a party in Boston and on the way home, Mary Ann's cough got worse. As they drove past Children's Hospital, Dad wanted to stop, but Mum insisted it would be a waste of time since the doctors already said to just keep her bundled up. That night Aunt Nell and Mum took turns trying to comfort Mary Ann as she was passed from one person to the next seated around the table. When she reached Mum, Mary Ann looked up at her and, through her incessant coughing, muttered, "I'm going home."

She died later that night. Dad felt it was Mum's fault and never forgave her.

Mum was a deeply religious woman. Her mother had taught her that God gives and God takes away. Reflecting on Mary Ann's final words, she came to believe that her daughter had told her that she was going home to Heaven. It's not for us to judge His actions or question His judgment, and she thus was able to deal with it better than Dad was.

She celebrated my birth, believing that I was a blessing and God's way of replacing what was taken from her. Dad, on the other hand, couldn't find the strength to accept what happened and wasn't able to cope with his grief. He seemed to distance himself from me, perhaps because he couldn't bear the thought of getting too close to another child for fear that history would repeat itself. The little time he spent with me, I think, was more of a distraction from his pain than a comfort to him.

My christening was a joyous occasion, filled with music, laughter and celebration for everyone but Dad. He was somber. The more gaiety spread around him, the worse he became. He couldn't escape the sudden death of Mary Ann. As time wore on, he slipped into deep depressions and drank heavily. Eventually, he lost his garage business in Beverly Farms. The death of his friend, Judge Holmes, around the same time probably was what clinched Dad's fate. Although remembered in the judge's will, Dad was too burdened with sorrow to resolve his problems. Sometime after my third birthday, he packed his bags and moved to Boston, leaving Mum to care for me alone.

Grandma Annie Coughlin had the foresight to invest in real estate shortly after arriving in America from Ireland years before I was born. She let us move into one of her cottages after Dad left when it became obvious that Mum would not be able to handle the rent by herself on our little Hart Street house.

It was near Halloween and the movers were loading the last of the furniture onto the truck from Hart Street. I was beside myself with excitement from all the commotion and kept trying to get a close-up, firsthand look at what was going on; I'm sure I got in the way at times. One of the movers turned his back to me and crouched down. I was mesmerized and couldn't take my eyes off of him. Suddenly he swung around. He was wearing a horrifyingly frightening mask.

"Boo!"

I screamed and ran as fast as my little legs could carry me into the house, into the kitchen and up on top of the kitchen table. I refused to budge. I just sat there screaming at the top of my lungs. Mum finally showed up after what seemed like an eternity and tried to console me.

"Now, now," she said. "It's not real. He was only fooling. He didn't mean to scare you like that. He was just playing. It's a Halloween mask — nothing to be afraid of."

It didn't work. I was branded for life. Call me a scaredy cat if you like, but that nightmare haunts me to this day.

Growing up with estranged parents was difficult. I cherished those times when Mum and I would visit with Dad, but found myself wishing we could live together.

Dad went to work for a wealthy New Englander named Mrs. Thayer. On some Sunday afternoons, Mum and I would catch the noon train to Boston and spend a few hours with him. I would watch holiday parades from the front living room of the Thayer mansion at 84 Beacon Street in the prestigious Back Bay of Boston. The house has since become a famous restaurant, the Hampshire House — famous because the bar in the restaurant was the setting for the television series "Cheers."

"No kid in Beverly Farms has this privilege," Dad would constantly remind me.

I didn't care. Privilege and wealth are adult concerns. Children are more concerned about basic things. All I wanted was to be a family. We could live in a shack for all I cared as long as we were together. And just once I wished I could hear either one of them say that they loved me. But that was not to be.

Mum went to work at the parish rectory as a live-in housekeeper when I was four, leaving me to live with Nana, Grandpa, and my three aunts, Nell, Eliza and Ann. Nell and I were very close through the years. She took me to tap dancing lessons and gave me my first perm in preparation for my class recital. Dad was furious with her for cutting my hair. He was working then at the Quincy Shipyard while living with an Irish family outside of Boston, and came for an occasional visit during weekends and holidays. Even though he wasn't a regular, ongoing part of my upbringing, he still tried to be controlling.

I entered first grade at St. Margaret's parochial school in 1939. When Nana and Nell finished getting me ready for my first day of school, they led me out the front door and pointed me up the street in the direction of St. Margaret's, several blocks away. I was one terrified little five-year-old slowly ambling my way all alone into the unknown. A sudden feeling of comfort overcame me like a warm blanket on a cold night when I got to the church hill and looked up to see Mum waiting outside the rectory to escort me to the classroom.

St. Margaret's was a small, eight-grade school with two grades in each room, staffed by the Sisters of Notre Dame de Namur. When Mum and I arrived in the classroom designated for first- and second-graders, we joined the other mothers and children standing scattered around the room. We waited. As my classroom teacher, Sister Ann, called out the names of the second-graders, they left their mother's side one by one and took a seat. Then it came time to seat the first-graders. Some started to cry. Being the youngest, I was last to be called. I started to tremble and my eyes welled with tears when I heard my name. Mum squeezed my hand. I looked at her as she gave me that stern glare which silently told me to control myself and do what I was told. Like a frightened little mouse, I slipped away from her and into my chair — the last seat in the last row.

As she left the room, Mum leaned over to me and whispered, "If you need to go to the bathroom, raise your hand and ask Sister."

"Yes Mum," I answered, still fighting back the tears.

She never heard me or, if she did, she didn't acknowledge it. She was already on her way into whatever awaited her beyond that door, leaving me once again to face the world alone. I couldn't understand why other children's moms would tell them they loved them while mine just reminded me to "sit up straight and behave yourself."

That feeling of loneliness amplified one day as winter approached. The days grew increasingly shorter and darkness set in by 4 p.m. We had to wait in line to be dismissed at the end of the school day. One day, I decided to be a chatterbox and was caught talking in line.

"Nancy! Zip it up," Sister Ann admonished. "Take your seat, young lady, and stay there until you make up your mind that you will not talk in class."

She led the rest of my classmates in the dismissal line out of the room and down the hallway. I started to cry. As I waited, the feeling of loneliness surrounding me began to intensify. It became eerily quiet. The only sounds to be heard came from my pounding little heart and the steady whimpering I could no longer control. I waited and waited, but Sister Ann didn't return.

"Maybe I should run home," I thought, as my heart thundered harder against my chest. "Surely Mum would understand. What could Sister Ann do to me if I left without telling her? Oh ... I don't want to know ..."

I was afraid to move.

It was so dark outside, I was immersed in blackness. The only light was the faint glow of the streetlight in front of the school. Had she left me here intentionally? Is this where I would spend the night?

"I bet Mum doesn't even realize I'm missing," I thought.

An eerieness crept inside me. Terror began to take hold followed by flashbacks of that Halloween and the mask. I was too frightened to do anything but sit there and sob.

Suddenly, a light in the corridor came on. I jumped. Too scared to scream, I curled up like a kitten as the classroom door swung open and the light switch flipped on. Sister Ann stood in the doorway, stunned. She never admitted it, but she had forgotten about me. She taught piano lessons after school, and after dismissing the rest of my class, had gone directly to her music session without giving me a second thought. Fortunately, evenings were getting seasonally chilly; she probably would not have found me had she not come back to the classroom to get her shawl to wear home to the convent.

"Are you still here, child?" she responded, then immediately called to her piano pupil. "Elizabeth, walk with Nancy to her grandmother's house on your way home, will you dear?"

I clung to Elizabeth as we stepped out into the cold and wouldn't let go of her until we were at Nana's house. I ran to the back door and into the kitchen. Mum was standing at the stove stirring soup. It was her day off from her job. Nana took in boarders, so Mum helped cook and serve the meals whenever she could. I clung to Mum's knees and sobbed as I relayed my terrifying experience to her. She never broke stride in her task of systematically churning the soup ladle, without offering one ounce of compassion or sympathy at my plight.

"The Sister must be right," she said, unemotionally. "You must have deserved being treated that way, otherwise she never would have punished you. The Sisters are always right. Don't you ever forget that!"

Monsignor Matthew Gleason was a warm, gentle, saintly priest whom everyone dearly loved. So dedicated was he to his parish and pastoral obligations that he never once took a day off during the entire thirty-five years of his priestly life in Beverly Farms. He grew fond of Mum and me. When I was seven years old, he invited me to move into the rectory. The Monsignor soon became the first significant male figure to have a lasting, positive influence on me.

That summer, I spent eight weeks at the Sisters camp in Tyngsboro, Massachusetts. Homesick and frightened, I cried all the way through every Sunday visit by family members during the entire two months I was away. What hurt most was that no one ever hugged me when they arrived or when they left. They would just say, "See you next visiting day," and leave without ever making physical contact with me. I would see other families touch each other and didn't understand why mine didn't. All I wanted was a hug.

Back in Beverly Farms, I went through a transformation. I gave up tap dance training and started taking piano lessons. Musical talent was common in our family. Dad's brother, Uncle Jerry O'Brien, was a renowned Irish accordionist in Boston who, during the 1930s and '40s, often toured on ocean liners between Boston and Ireland as part of the ship's entertainment. My cousin, Johnny Sullivan, also a prominent accordionist of the era, played for private parties given by the Kennedys and McCormacks of Boston. Even Dad played the accordion, and Mum, although she never took a formal lesson, could play the piano by ear. I must have inherited that trait from her, because I had a natural flare for music. During my first three years of piano training, I never learned a scale or heard of a chord. My teacher was a sickly nun who didn't bother to edify such basics. I never had the opportunity to practice, but I also never missed a lesson and always gave 100 percent effort, which paid off. I remember how Mum sat proudly in the audience wearing the new hat she bought for each of my annual recitals.

Grandpa had a contracting business. During the winter, he rented out his pung, a low, box kind of toboggan pulled by a horse, to local wealthy people for sleigh rides. I sometimes prankishly tried to sneak my friends onto the pung as he exercised the horses in preparation for these hired excursions, but he always caught us. He refused to let us take free jaunts out of concern for injury liability, not out of meanness.

Grandpa died the same year I entered St. Mary's High School in Beverly. Mum's brother, John, was always good to me. He managed trucks that plowed snow on state roads, and also was in charge of several of Grandpa's trucks, which cleared private driveways for local estates. Uncle John made me the envy of my friends by teaching me how to drive the smaller truck with a stick shift around the farms.

When Grandpa died, Nell took over as administrator of the business, while continuing her nursing duties at the local hospital. She was well-known as a nurse in the small community, and was extremely popular for her generosity to neighbors in the small town.

In 1947, I became a teenager, with all the trials and tribulations of youth, such as boy infatuations and smoking on the sly. The first time I ventured to smoke was when my friend, Charlotte, and I swiped grapes from the Bradley's estate. We lit up a cigar amongst the grapevines and both became agonizingly ill. However, once the color returned to my cheeks and the queasiness in my stomach subsided, the rebellion continued, but I switched to a less potent tobacco product, enticing some of the older kids to buy Pall Mall cigarettes for me. They were the longest and cheapest cigarettes available. I buried them in the backyard each day so Mum wouldn't find them. After getting away with this for two years, I became a bit lackadaisical and a little more brazen. One rainy day I decided not to chance getting my precious commodities wet and opted to keep them tucked away in my slicker pocket. That was the day I got caught.

By then I was fifteen and very much aware of boys. Although I'd never taken an organ lesson, I started playing for Benediction two nights a week and for the Men's Choir practice one night a week. After practice, I and some of the men in the choir would flirt.

"Hey, Nance, how 'bout comin' to the library with us?"

Knowing that the "library" was what they called the local pub, I would counter with something like, "Why bother? You must have read every book in there by now."

New England's severe winters can be brutal, and Beverly Farms, situated on the coast, got more than its share of blizzards. Grandpa's business often had to hire some of the local boys to help out by steering plows or assisting the drivers in clearing snow. I would spend the nights at Nana's with a couple of my girlfriends, brewing tea and keeping the cocoa hot for the boys on the plows. We girls always felt this service was in our best interest — a smart investment.

Living at the rectory was beginning to interfere with my expanding social life. Mum forbade me to date during high school, so I had to find ways to sneak around her. It was a challenge, but I always came up with some sort of excuse to get out — like going to the movies with a girlfriend or to a school ballgame. By the third year of high school, I began staying at the homestead on weekends because Mum didn't want to leave the lights on outside the rectory after 9 p.m. Nell was like an older sister to me during this time. She covered up for me and repeatedly came to my defense whenever Mum became suspicious or made an issue about my socializing. Her vocabulary was choice and relentlessly to the point.

"Goddammit, let the kid do as she wants," was her retort when standing up for me.

Aunt Ann got married during the summer of that year and took over the third floor of the homestead. Around the same time, one of my cousins got married. I served as one of her bridesmaids. The wedding turned out to be one of the turning points in my life, marking my transition into the dating scene. A petite boy usher with the bluest eyes imaginable served as my partner. That's how I met my first love. Bobby D eventually became my first steady boyfriend.

By then I had my driver's license, and Monsignor Gleason allowed me to use his big, beautiful Buick at least once a month. I don't think that courtesy would have lasted long if he'd found out some of the things I did with it. For example, Bobby would sometimes buy a case of beer, which we stored in the trunk of Monsignor's car, praying that he would never get a flat or have a reason to open the trunk. Fortunately, he drove his car only to get a haircut once a month, so our little escapade was never exposed. We rarely had much money. Some Friday nights, we would drive to John's Pizza in Beverly, spend fifty cents for a pizza to go, eat it in the car, drive to the drugstore for a glass of water, then use our last quarter to buy gas to cruise around looking for friends.

Babysitting was a really big thing in those days. There were a lot of wealthy families in the area who lived in beautiful mansions. These were popular jobs with the teenage crowd. Usually, there was little food to feed the children, but plenty of booze was always on hand. Once the little ones were bathed and bedded, the party began.

Things started getting strenuous. I had a new Sister as a piano instructor and she immediately established a pattern of dishing out tough assignments. Plus, Monsignor Gleason kept encouraging me to play the organ full time. I kept refusing, but he eventually took his request to Mum. Almost overnight I became not only the full-time organist, but also the choir director. The burden was almost unbearable. I never got over the feeling of inadequacy from being the youngest in all my classes. I think starting school at such an early age was a mistake that tormented me throughout my life. I always felt inadequate and couldn't help notice that I always seemed to be at the bottom of the class academically. The fact that I struggled with Latin just compounded these resentments and made overcoming the obstacles facing me even more difficult. I finally managed to convince Mum that I just couldn't cope with a 50-male choir, organ, piano, and schoolwork. She allowed me to give up piano lessons and arranged for me to be tutored in Latin.

My senior year in high school was particularly stressful. Nana suffered a fatal heart attack on January 1, 1951. I experienced other separations — too many for my fragile psyche — but this one was particularly difficult for me to cope with. A certain amount of hope is always attached to separations — hope that whatever caused the separation will be mended and a reuniting of what once was will take place. With death, especially death of a special loved one, there is the realization that this separation is permanent, at least in this life.

To add to my anxieties, I was facing graduation and had to contend with leaving home, setting goals, and establishing what my future lifestyle would become. I had to decide what I wanted to do with my life.

Bobby and I had been going steady for more than a year, and we were talking about such things as a friendship ring and marriage. Mum had no idea that this relationship existed, and with the help of some, like Nell, I did a pretty good job of concealing it from her. She came home from a party one night and was astonished at having learned what she assumed was a rumor floating about town.

"Nance," she confided in me, "do you know what the latest gossip is?"

"No," I answered, holding my breath.

"You're going steady with Bobby D."

I almost dropped the cocoa I was making.

"You're kidding," I replied. "Isn't that a riot?"

I was afraid she might see through my feeble attempt to treat it like a joke by acting blasé. I don't know if she believed me or not, but she seemed satisfied and dropped the subject.

The fact that all of my classmates had made decisions about college or jobs didn't ease my frustrations. I was getting pressured from all sides about what I was going to be doing the next year.

"White Splendor," a play about Our Lady of Fatima, was a repeat school production from our freshman year. All music pupils, past and present, were required to participate in the religious play about the appearance of our Blessed Mother to three small shepherd children in 1917 near Fatima, Portugal, giving them a message to deliver to the world. This message became known as the "Peace Plan from Heaven," a warning to us to pray the Rosary every day. If we didn't, there would be a third and more terrible world war.

I played the youngest child, Jacinta, sister of Francisco and cousin of Lucia, the oldest of the three. Jacinta was outgoing and energetic, and loved to dance. I easily identified with her. When the apparitions of the Queen of Heaven occurred, Lucia swore the others to secrecy, but Jacinta couldn't contain herself and, bubbling over with excitement of their experience, told her family, who in turn told the village. Controversy, mockery, skepticism and anger followed, so much so that Jacinta promised never to reveal another secret. She kept her promise even after the vision of hell was given to them in the third apparition. This vision seemed to affect Jacinta the most.

"Jesus wishes to make use of you to have me acknowledged and loved," the Blessed Mother told them. "He wishes to establish in the world devotion to my Immaculate Heart."

This was more than a revelation to me. It was a calling. The play brought to the surface deep feelings that had been stirring inside me for some time. I began to feel a strong pull toward a religious life that required entering the convent. I really didn't want to go into the Sisterhood, but I couldn't escape this overpowering calling that was so very strong and persistent.

Fortunately, Sister Patricia was a music teacher I had grown to admire. She was a tall, beautiful, gentle nun who looked absolutely magnificent in her habit, so much so that I often fantasized about whether or not I could look that good in the garb. I confided to her that I was considering entering the convent someday. She reminded me that there were two entrance days each year — one in February and one in August; all I had to do was make a choice. It was April of 1951 and the options were spinning in my head like a carousel that goes on forever: pursue music ... marry Bobby ... become a nun ... find a job ... stay with Bobby ... join the convent ... become a hair dresser ... marry Bobby ... play music ... join the convent ... marry Bobby ... work as a telephone operator ... become a nun. Round and round and round they went. The convent became more and more dominant as the cycle continued to churn. I had been carrying the secret of wanting to enter the convent for several months, and one day Sister Patricia intervened.

"Go home now," she said, "tell your mom and come back to me with the news."

I did as she suggested. It was Friday afternoon. Mum was resting on the bed. I put on her new fur, paraded into the bedroom, viewed myself in the mirror and tried to strike a nonchalant pose.

"Mum, you've been bugging me about what I'm doing next year," I blurted out, loudly and emphatically. "Well, I'd like to go into the convent, but I'm not sure when!"

I didn't wait for a response. I immediately ran out of the bedroom and down the stairs. I flung the coat on a chair as I raced out of the rectory and back to school.

Sister Patricia was there waiting for me.

"I did it!" I proclaimed. "I told her!"

"What was her reaction?"

"I don't know," I gasped. "I didn't wait for an answer!"

It didn't matter. It was done. I had broken the ice and made the commitment. A certain sense of relief came over me. Someone in the family finally knew. Now I could get on with making plans. Still, there were others to inform — friends, aunts, Dad, and oh yes, Bobby.

It took a while for the news to clearly register with Mum. She had secretly prayed for so long for me to get a calling from the Lord that it startled her when I blurted out that her prayers had actually been answered. A peaceful resolve also came over her. She had always felt that the Lord had a special reason for taking her baby, Mary Ann, to be with Him, and now He was going to protect her other daughter, making her safe from the world through her vows to Him.

I asked Mum to keep the secret until I had a chance to prepare myself for breaking the news, knowing full well that she would have to be the one to tell Dad. Bobby D was my biggest dilemma. We were talking about a friendship ring for graduation, and now I would have to hit him with this. He was my major conflict. How could I tell him? Did I really want to enter the convent? How could I leave him?

Mum didn't keep the secret for long. She surreptitiously and, I'm sure, proudly divulged my plans to Aunt Nell, who was not overjoyed at the news. Nell remained against the idea from the onset. Monsignor Gleason was also given the scoop since Mum felt a strong obligation to him for being so good to us over the years.

Several weeks later, Sister Patricia, who I thought was the only one who knew at the time, pulled me aside to suggest that I approach my senior teacher, Sister Rose, as she would be the one who would have to make the official recommendation to the convent.

The nuns positioned themselves in a certain area during the changing of classes to prevent us from talking in the halls. I was reluctant, as usual, but finally got the nerve to make a move and approached Sister Rose one day as she stood in the corridor.

"Sister Rose, I'd like to go to the convent, but I'm not sure if it will be August or February," I blurted out in passing, without breaking stride as I continued to my next class.

She was waiting for me at her post in the corridor when the class ended.

"Nancy, don't you think you had better wait a year and simmer down? I don't think you'll persevere!"

She was well aware of us Farms girls' reputations. We were always getting into some kind of trouble — typing notes in class to our boyfriends, hollering out the windows when they arrived to pick us up, skipping classes to get caught up on homework. We stuck together and were considered to be the free spirits of St. Mary's High. There was Mary Sanphy, Maria Campagnola, Lena Zampell, Ann Kelly and, of course, me.

Sister Rose felt I was incapable of adjusting to convent life. She thought I was too wild to settle down. I was indignant. No one was going to tell me that I wouldn't make it. She just reaffirmed my decision, making me so adamant that I wanted to go as soon as possible — in August.

Monsignor Degan, pastor of the high school, interviewed all seniors before graduation. He had a typed list containing each senior's anticipated destination on the desk in front of him so that he could relate directly to each student during the interrogation. I was in and out rather quickly compared to the others. Although my visit with him was brief, I could clearly see the sheet with information about my classmates.

Mary Samphy and Mary Weir were my two best friends. We did everything together — movies, record hops, basketball games. They emerged shocked from what they had learned, apparently having seen his paper indicating that I would be going to the convent. This meant the end of our little three-way friendship, that we would soon be separated for a long time — perhaps forever. As disturbing as it was to see them so upset, I still felt a strange sort of relief that they knew.

"Please don't tell Bobby," I begged them. "I want to tell him myself."

It didn't work. The word spread rapidly and Bobby soon found out. To make matters worse, when he tried to call me at the rectory, he was told I wasn't there. When the news became common knowledge, various people took the posture of protecting me from worldly pleasures . Bobby was considered to be one of my "worldly pleasures." Monsignor Gleason was among my protectors.

When Bobby and I finally did connect, he was shocked.

"Is it true?" he wanted to know.

"Yes."

"Why didn't you tell me right away?"

"I wanted to, Bobby. I tried to, but, you know me, I wanted to wait until just the right moment."

"The right moment? What do you mean, the right moment?"

"I just wanted to — oh, I don't know what I mean. You mean so much to me, Bobby, I just wanted to share the good news with you, not devastate you this way."

"I can't believe it ..."

"I didn't want to hurt you."

"Well, you did," he said. "This really hurts. I don't understand ..."

"It's not you, Bobby, you must believe that. I do love you, but this is a calling from God. I can't explain it, but it's something I just have to do."

"How can you say that you love me in the same breath that you tell me you're going to leave me? It doesn't make sense."

"It's a calling, Bobby. Can't you see that? God called me and I must answer."

His initial shock turned to anger, then to confusion, and finally he began to sob softly.

"I could never say good-bye to you, Nancy."

"This is so hard for me, Bobby. My heart aches. I feel like it's torn in two between you and God. I don't want to lose you, but I have to follow my faith, and my faith tells me to answer God's calling, and He will take care of everything. I must believe that."

"And I must believe that I will never see you again. I can't live with that. I can't bear to watch you leave me this way. I have to be the one to leave."

"What are you talking about?"

"I'm going to sign up for the Navy right away."

We spent the entire summer re-enacting this dialogue over and over again. It was painful for both of us. I found myself repeatedly trying to explain this calling, which Bobby tried to understand but couldn't. I found myself telling him that I loved him and yet I was giving him up. It didn't make sense to him, nor did it to me. I just knew that I had to do it.

I had taken a summer job as a live-in babysitter for the Wigglesworths on their estate near the ocean. One day while there, the phone rang. It was Mum.

"Your dad called. He's blaming me for you entering the convent."

I met with Dad to discuss the matter. He perceived this decision as an escape from my situation, attributed to our broken family. He felt a certain amount of guilt for having left me when I was three, but most of his criticism was directed at Mum for leaving me to go to work when I was four. As much as I tried to explain that this was something spiritual, something that was directed and inspired by Divine Intervention, he insisted that I was simply "leaving to find a home."

Mum became concerned about raising the money necessary to send me away. The convent would cost $500 for a dowry, $200 for board and another $200 for entrance trousseau. She worried for nothing. The town threw a farewell party for me on July 26 and collected more than $1,000 to cover my expenses. It was a grand party. All of my relatives were there with their accordions.

I think everyone assumed that I wouldn't last long in the convent. Actually, I don't think many wanted me to go in the first place. In fact, I believe Mum and Sister Patricia were the only ones who prayed that I would stay once I entered. In all honesty, I had my own doubts about whether I would be able to last long. I inadvertently exposed my reservations to Bobby on the eve of his departure to go into the military.

It was July 27 — our last night together — and we had fried clams for dinner at a seafood restaurant in Essex. It was an uneventful evening, not what one would expect from a couple very much in love and about to separate, perhaps for the last time. Most of our conversation was a replay of the ongoing debate we had from the time I announced my intention of joining the convent. He didn't understand it and I couldn't explain it.

"It's not easy, Bobby" I said to him. "It's the most difficult thing I've ever done. And I don't know if this is going to work out for me or not. I just know I've got to answer the call and do what my heart tells me to do. That same heart, by the way, that is broken because part of it belongs to you."

He just looked forlornly at me. Then suddenly I let it slip.

"Look," I said, "I don't know, it may turn out to be a mistake and I may be back here in six months."

The tiny glimmer in his eyes was the only time he showed the slightest sign of pleasure since all this talk about the convent arose. He may have interpreted it totally different from the way I meant it. I had reservations, doubts about myself — not about whether or not it was the right thing to do. And certainly not because my love for Bobby was stronger than my love for God.

He just stared at me and quietly mumbled, "Well, we'll see," but I could sense the tinge of hope that my words had given him.

Early the next morning, he left for Great Lakes, Illinois, to start Navy boot camp. Three days later, I headed off for training school in Waltham, Massachusetts, to prepare for becoming a nun.

Growing up truly is hard to do.

Entering the Convent

S t. Julie Billiart, an eighteenth century Frenchwoman, founded the religious family of the Sisters of Notre Dame. St. Julie, born July 12, 1751 in the small village of Cuvilly in the ancient province of Picardy in Northern France, was a simple, sickly woman who hailed from an impoverished family. She survived the French Revolution and the Reign of Terror, which saw many of her friends face the guillotine, and yet she stood erect for France and for the Church. Her faith was indelible and her indomitable spirit led to the formation of the first Sisters of Notre Dame in February 1804. In May of that same year, she experienced a complete cure of the paralysis that had plagued her for twenty-two years. Her image of God was one of both mystery and goodness. Her recognition of God's goodness was the hallmark of her common sense wisdom, a trademark that became characteristic of the Sisters of Notre Dame de Namur and the guidepost for my future.

"O God, you blessed your daughter Julie with humility and wisdom in the midst of struggle and misunderstanding. Through her, many women and men came to know your love and goodness towards us. Bless all those who follow in her footsteps, that we may continue the work of showing your goodness to everyone, a work that you began in her. We ask this in the names of Jesus and Mary. Amen."

It was raining, damp and cold the morning of August 1, 1951 — Entrance Day, the day I entered the sisters of Notre Dame training school in Waltham, Massachusetts. Three full carloads of family and friends accompanied me on the hour-long drive to Waltham. I arrived fully decked out in my postulant dress and cape, black shoes and stockings, and joined the other thirty-two girls who entered that day. We were all capped in the afternoon — a black net cap was placed on our head to complete our uniform and signify that we were officially recognized as postulants.

At 4 p.m. a bell, sounding like a gigantic fire alarm, announced the time for all visitors to leave and the postulants to assemble upstairs. Tears began to flow. Mother was the happiest one there and tried to bolster everyone's spirits.

"No tears or good-byes," she cheerily sang. "We'll see you next month."

No one could stop Dad's tears. He sobbed out loud and pleaded with me to come home.

"I'll give you anything," he begged, "a Lincoln Continental and a trip to Ireland — anything you want, but please come back."

At times during the next few days, I wished I had taken him up on his offer. Those first days were like being in prison. We were all crammed into a small room adorned with nothing but a couple of statues and hard straight-back chairs to sit on. We were assigned seats and frisked to make sure we didn't have any contraband — candy, cigarettes, money. For three days, we just sat like little kindergartners, staring at each other and whispering.

Sister Ann, the mistress of postulants, spoke with us for about an hour each day. She kept making a point about the rule of silence that we would be keeping. What an ominous phrase that is — the Great Silence Rule — to be said in front of a teenager. I started to suspect that perhaps Sister

Rose was right in her predictions that I wouldn't last long. Those first few days indoctrinating us to all the rules that we had to abide by from that time forth were enough to discourage the most diehard zealot. After the third day the indoctrination was over and a whole new rigid existence began.

We weren't allowed in the chapel at all for a week until we learned how to walk in a line and genuflect. Once there, we were allowed to leave only when the mistress of postulants gave a knock on the bench, signaling our departure in unison.

Sister Ann was extremely strict and quite the taskmaster. The first volunteered penance we were taught to say was the rosary, a common devotion to Mother Mary, with our arms extended on the first, third and fifth decades. Other forms of penance followed, such as kneeling to kiss the floor when making the Way of the Cross on the third, fifth and seventh station.

Every night, we filled a basin in the common lavatory and brought it to our cells in the dormitory, where we spread a mat on the floor and washed. Four postulants slept in a dorm. Each bed was enclosed completely with curtains — the closest to privacy we had. We were eventually allowed to take one bath a week at an assigned time and day.

My daily routine was so set and so rigid that I led a robotic existence. If asked what I did on any specific day, my answer would be the same.

At 5 a.m. we rose. At 5:30, we spent an hour in the chapel meditating, and at 6:30 we attended Mass. At 7:30, we had breakfast in silence. From 8 to 8:45 we had our daily charges, and from 9 to 9:45 we said the rosary and a spiritual reading in the chapel. From 9:45 to 10:15, we consumed a drink and snack, in silence, and went to classes from 10:15 to 11:45, at which time we returned to the chapel for an examination of conscience. Our big meal, dinner, took place at noon until cleanup at 12:45 p.m., all in silence. Our first half hour recreation, one of only two occasions during the day in which we could speak, occurred from 1 and 1:30, after which we returned to classes and studied until 4 p.m. After another half-hour snack and tea period, again in silence, we spent fifteen minutes in chapel praying. Study hour was from 5 to 6 p.m., followed by a half hour of Holy Family sewing or learning about the institute. From 6:30 to 7 p.m., we meditated, after which we had a light supper lasting forty-five minutes, with fifteen minutes cleaning up afterwards. At 8 we enjoyed our second, and final, recreation of the day during which we could talk. Night prayers were then held in chapel from 8:30 to 8:45, after which we returned to our dorms. Lights out came with a knock in the corridor at 9:30.

Every day was identical to the one before. The routine was repeated every single day, day in and day out, seven days a week, fifty two weeks a year, for three years. Few variations from this schedule ever occurred. Sometimes, if it was hot in the chapel in the summer, Sister Ann would allow us to meditate in the garden. On Sundays, except for Advent and Lent, we were allowed to speak at meals. After we sat down at the table, the mistress would start the meal by saying, "Praise be Jesus Christ," to which we would answer "Amen," and proceed to chatter away. She would signal us to stop talking by passing her plate at the end of the meal.

It was difficult to get to know our fellow postulants; we were all so busy learning rules and being punished for breaking them. Still, we were a close group despite our lack of verbal communication. The discipline amid silence actually created a common bond that united us. The first postulant to leave did so during the first week because she couldn't tolerate all the bells — electric bells on a timer, outside chimes, bells for class, bells for prayer, bells for chores; bells, bells, bells, the only times the sounds of silence were broken, the incessant ringing of bells.

We were allowed one visit a month — on an assigned Sunday — from four members of the family. If five came, we had to forfeit the next month's visit. On one such visit, two of my former classmates rode up with my mother and aunts, bringing my total number of visitors over the limit. Inadvertently, I bolted over to see them when spotting them in the car and was immediately sent to see Sister Ann. I was told that they would have to sit in the car or I would forfeit my next visit. I had merely forgotten the rule during my excitement at seeing old friends, but the jolt of being rapidly yanked so publicly back into my current reality in front of family and friends was disconcerting. I felt like the Germans must have felt with the Gestapo — no longer free, and spied on at every turn.

My cousin Bill Maciel, Aunt Liza's son, would come along with his mom, but he wasn't included in the maximum count. He was allowed to visit with the others because he was so little.

Strict adherence to visitors was only one small part of the totalitarian regime under which I now lived. All of our mail, both incoming and outgoing, was censored. Beds had to be totally stripped each morning at 5. No pillowcases were used, so we pulled our bedsheets over the pillows when making the bed. The mistress inspected beds after breakfast for square corners, taut, unwrinkled sheets, etc. Entering our dorm at night, we often found our beds pulled apart because of poor corners and wrinkles. Numerous times we discovered the light bulb missing from the center of the dorm because the last postulant out in the morning had forgotten to turn the switch off; all four of us were punished by having to dress and undress in the dark for a week, or however long the mistress felt it would take us to learn responsibility.

We were instructed never to reveal to our monthly visitors what we were fed. This became awkward and difficult, because my family always asked what I had for dinner and I couldn't tell them. Dad was convinced they were feeding us only bread and water. That wasn't true, but I couldn't correct him. So, I had to let him believe what he wanted to, although the reality of gaining about 25 pounds the first three months I was there made it obvious I was being fed well. In fact, we were fed extremely well, five times a day. Still, they persisted in bringing up the issue. I couldn't take the constant inquisition and finally blurted out our menu during one of their visits. My adjustment into the Sisterhood apparently was working, because I felt so guilty that night I couldn't sleep.

Food, or rather the abundance of it, in fact, became my enemy. My first true test of faith came in the fourth month. And it had to do with food. Our meals were fit for lumberjacks. Suddenly one morning at breakfast, I just couldn't eat. Refusing to eat was not allowed. We were never permitted to decline anything when it was passed to us. I sat with all this food on my plate, my stomach in knots, unable to get a morsel down. There were four long tables in the refectory where we ate and several of my colleagues began to help me out by allowing me to slip them muffins or hard-boiled eggs under the table. A number of times I managed to sneak food into the large pockets in my habit and flush it down the toilet at the end of the meal. My little clandestine operation worked fairly well until my turn came to sit next to the mistress. That was pure agony. Mornings were the worst. One day she forced me to stay at the table until 2 in the afternoon to finish my dinner. After a few weeks I couldn't take anymore. It got so bad that the mere rattling of dishes or smell of food before a meal would turn my stomach. I mustered up my courage to approach Sister Ann and ask permission to lessen my food intake. She refused. I started to get ill at the table and would head for the bathroom. She tolerated it for a few days, but then forbade me to leave the table. My reaction to food had a reciprocal effect on the others and two other sisters began demonstrating the same problem. Our nerves played havoc with us. We developed a pattern of gulping our food, then forcing ourselves to keep it down. While they were somewhat empathetic with our dilemma, the other sisters found this ritual to be amusing and started referring to us as "The Gulpers" at recreation. They teased us relentlessly.

Christmas was approaching. The Mother General arrived from Namur, Belgium, for her first visit to the United States in twelve years. One of her initial observations was that Americans did not enjoy hearty breakfasts, so she immediately added one more item to our breakfast menu — hot cereal! Christmas Day was the last straw. I couldn't cope with this food quandary any longer. Food was consuming me, instead of the other way around. The dilemma of dealing with food had become unbearable. I had no choice but to, once again, beg Sister Ann for permission to lessen my food intake. She sarcastically told me I'd have to ask the Mother General for that permission and, ignoring my plea, sat down to dinner. Because my assigned seat was at another table out of her sight, I managed to eat nothing but an olive for dinner without getting caught. I continued this little deception every chance I could. It was effective enough that, by supper each night, it became a bit easier for me to eat. Still, it was affecting my state of mind and I couldn't help but question my resolve in the determination to be a nun.

About the only thing that helped to boost my morale during all this anxiety over food was being asked, with three other postulants, to teach piano lessons once a week to local students. Fridays after the 4 p.m. bread-and-honey-in silence, all four of us traveled through the tunnel connecting the living quarters of the Sisters to the classroom building to give piano lessons to students attending a local school. I really enjoyed this. I absolutely relished the chance to communicate with the outside world. But the real icing on the cake was being able to do something that I truly loved — play the piano.

Still, my food problem, combined with the militant mistress, made me uncertain about wanting to remain in the convent. One day I learned during a visit from home that Bobby D had been medically discharged from the Navy. He had returned to Beverly Farms for a fresh start. I went stammering and stuttering to Sister Ann.

"Sister, I ... uh, decided that I can't ... uh, that I'm not, uh, cut out for this ... and ... uh, have reconsidered being a nun. I, uh ... that is, uh ... after careful consideration ... I mean ... that is to say, uh ... I've come to the conclusion ... rather, I, uh ... I ... I want to leave the convent."

She just stared at me and said, "Nonsense. You're just tired. Go back to your quarters and take a nap."

Taking a Sunday nap was unheard of in those days. The next day I was handed a copy of St. John of the Cross, in which he described the dark night of the soul:

Wherein the soul sings of the happy chance which it had in passing through the dark night of faith, in detachment and purgation of itself, to union with the Beloved.

1. On a dark night, Kindled in love with yearnings — oh, happy chance! —

I went forth without being observed, My house being now at rest.

2. In darkness and secure, By the secret ladder, disguised — oh, happy chance! — In darkness and in concealment, My house being now at rest.

3. In the happy night, In secret, when none saw me, Nor I beheld aught, Without light or guide, save that which burned in my heart.

4. This light guided me More surely than the light of noonday, To the place where he (well I knew who!) was awaiting me — A place where none appeared.

5. Oh, night that guided me, Oh, night more lovely than the dawn, Oh, night that joined Beloved with lover, Lover transformed in the Beloved!

6. Upon my flowery breast, Kept wholly for himself alone, There he stayed sleeping, and I caressed him, And the fanning of the cedars made a breeze.

7. The breeze blew from the turret As I parted his locks; With his gentle hand he wounded my neck And caused all my senses to be suspended.

8. I remained, lost in oblivion; My face I reclined on the Beloved. All ceased and I abandoned myself, Leaving my cares forgotten among the lilies.

"What you are experiencing is a temptation," Sister Ann explained. "It will pass."

She was relentless and harsh and loved to rule the nest. There was no way that she would allow one of her subjects to just get up and walk out.

On visiting day, Monsignor Gleason always sent along with Mum $25 enclosed in an envelope with something funny typed on it. He knew how much I loved shoes, so one week he innocently scribbled on the envelope, "to buy a pair of red shoes." It made Sister Ann so irate that she could hardly contain herself.

"What do you think you're doing asking for shoes?" she reprimanded. "If you need anything, ask ME! If I feel you need it, I will see that you get it. Do you understand?"

"Yes, Sister."

Couldn't she tell it was a joke? How could a nun wear red shoes with a black-and-white habit? Besides, we had to relinquish any and all gifts to the Superior, so why would I make such a request?

Monsignor Gleason visited often with his curate. Mum came along for the ride hoping to sneak in an extra visit. The Monsignor was a generous benefactor of the Sisters of Notre Dame, so they never refused him anything. He would usually ask the portress — the nun assigned to greet visitors at the door — to get permission for Mum to come in and say hello after he and I had visited in a private parlor for a while. These special visitations made me nervous, knowing that the other postulants didn't enjoy such privileges. Plus, I would have to make up any work I missed back in the postulate, so I didn't get pleasure from these special advantages as I perhaps should have.

I was too frightened to approach the mistress again and ask for dismissal, but I wanted to leave so badly that I told a couple of my friends I was plotting an escape to a local gas station, where I'd call Aunt Nell to come and get me. I knew Nell would back me up, but Mum would definitely try to talk me into staying. I was so confident my plan would work that I skipped my weekly assigned bath, saying to myself, "I'll be home this week, so I'll wait."

It was a cold day in January, with several inches of snow on the ground. I had just flushed a boiled egg and huge slice of home-baked bread down the toilet after breakfast. I decided to once again confront the mistress about leaving. Wrapped in the traditional black shawl that nuns wore in winter as outer garments, I made my way past the laundry door, where another postulant stopped me.

"Don't do this," she pleaded. "Please don't go this way. Turn back. Don't give up. I don't want you to leave."

I felt so helpless at that point. I had no money, no support of my decision, and I was frightened of authority. I had no choice. I turned back and went to chapel. I asked the Lord to help me escape.

That week, the canonical examiner came to interview each postulant in preparation for our entering the novitiate and taking the habit of the Sisters of Notre Dame. Monsignor Reilly's obligation was to ensure no one was being forced into the novitiate. The novitiate was the Sisters' first big step in religious life, pronouncing the first vows.

Monsignor Reilly also was responsible for witnessing us signing our will. We were free to leave our prior belongings to anyone we desired, but if we acquired anything after vows, those assets would be left to the order.

When it came my time to be interviewed, I walked silently, yet anxiously, through the tunnel from the postulate to the professed parlors.

"How am I going to answer this priest when he asks if I want to be a Sister of Notre Dame?" I thought.

The meeting was brief. The Monsignor was methodical and asked all the pertinent questions that were required of him. He also witnessed the signing of my will, but never asked the key question I expected. Perhaps he simply assumed that since I was there, I desired to become a Sister. On the other hand, I didn't volunteer any opposition to that assumption.

I was at my desk trying to study epistemology, a complex subject dealing with the theory of the nature and grounds of knowledge, when I realized an inner influence was guiding me. It was the same force I had experienced the previous spring, directing me to the convent. I was being driven by some ever-present, unknown power. I didn't know what it was, only that it was overpoweringly real — perhaps Nana or Mary Ann, already in Heaven experiencing the grandeur of it all, reaching out to guide me. It was the strongest energy I've ever felt and I knew that I had no choice but to obey.

We prepared to enter the novitiate. An institute number was given to each of us — mine was 573 — to sew into all of our clothes. Plus, we had to submit three names to determine our new Christian moniker, which would remain with us forever. My first choice was Sister Marie Timothy in respect of my mother and father. I tried to use a form of Matthew in tribute to Monsignor Gleason, but it was already taken.

Sister Ann hounded me constantly about biting my nails. I'm sure this was one of the telltale signs of insecurity and a lack of love that I grew up with, but the habitual tendency had been with me most of my life. The stress of the strict discipline and anxieties surrounding the routine at the postulate exacerbated my nail-biting. Her harassment didn't help. She finally told me that I would not be allowed to don the nun's habit if I continued to engage in this practice. Somehow I managed to overcome it and quit.

There was an eight-day retreat — nothing but absolute silence and prayers for eight days and nights — in preparation for entering the novitiate. This was an opportunity to completely isolate ourselves from the world and concentrate solely on the new direction we were about to embark upon. About midway through the retreat, we were brought before the Provincial Superior individually to ask permission to enter the novitiate. Still torn between the two forces of wanting to continue and wanting to quit, I avoided the question throughout the interview. She finally opted to press the issue.

"Why did you come to see me?"

That inner force compelling me to proceed suddenly took charge.

"Sister Provincial, may I have the habit of the Sisters of Notre Dame?" rolled from my unsuspecting lips.

On the eighth and final day of this first retreat, all of us who remained marched from our dormitories down the corridor, decked out in long black dresses that had been made to fit, with long black aprons. At one point in the dormitory, our hair was cut off in lengthy strips and wrapped in newspaper for our trunk. We then proceeded to the left wing of the corridor into the bathroom where another professed sister shaved our heads with an electric shaver. That's why the long strands of hair were saved — in the event that we left the order, we could have enough hair to make a wig until our natural hair grew back.

Panic time! I had no idea that this would happen. As kids, we never suspected the nuns in school had shaved heads under those headpieces. Their heads were always covered. Now I knew why. I was devastated. My beautiful feather cut brunette hair with its highly noticeable and distinctive bleached streak was gone — all gone.

Once the first part of our headpieces, the band, was placed on our heads and a white veil was draped over our arms, we proceeded in line to the chapel for the official ceremony. It was a truly uplifting, religious experience, filled with the sort of sacred beauty that remains in the deepest recesses of memory for a lifetime. Organ music filled the chambers with a solemn ambience befitting the occasion, while bells added a taste of tradition to the majestic experience. A magnificent choir of more than 100 sisters sang jubilant hymns as we proceeded toward the altar. The Sister Provincial placed a veil on our headpiece and gave us a large rosary to be hung down from our waist. The kiss of peace from all the Sisters in the chapel followed, and one by one our names were presented. It was like a rebirth. From that moment on I was known as Sister Marie Timothy.

That evening we were allowed to enjoy recreation for supper and exchange reactions to the day. The following morning we moved our few belongings into the novitiate wing. I was so nervous in my new surroundings and in my fresh, new habit that I got sick all over my brand new apron. Fortunately, our new mistress was more understanding and kinder than Sister Ann, so my behavior wasn't interpreted as misconduct or rebellion or a lack of control relative to this latest change. The transition, therefore, wasn't accompanied by the sort of punishment to which I had grown accustomed.

The second phase of my training was about to commence.

The Novitiate

Emmanuel College is a highly prestigious, co-educational, Catholic liberal arts college in Boston founded by the Sisters of Notre Dame de Namur in 1919. We novices were automatically enrolled there and assigned a curriculum designed to thoroughly prepare us for teaching. We had no choice as to which courses we would take, at least in the early years. Our program was mapped out for us.

Our overall schedule in the novitiate was much the same as the postulate, except that we had more course work and the classes were extremely difficult. The difference between us and other students at Emmanuel was that we didn't have the luxury of being on campus to interact with classmates. Sisters came from Boston to teach us at the novitiate. These two strict years were to be our canonical years.

There were new rules and penances to learn. It seemed we had to ask permission for everything — from the routine to the usual, mundane to the bizarre. Permission had to be obtained to go to the dorm, to use a restroom, to visit another floor, or to rinse out underwear or hankies — everything. We were never allowed to get up at night to use the lavatory. This was all meant to teach us to be humble and submissive. We always tried to find ways to circumvent these restrictions and shared our ideas with one another during recreation. Once I got up around 2 a.m. and waited for a train to pass by on the nearby tracks so I could slip through my dorm door into the lav without being heard. I then sat there quietly waiting for the next train in order to flush the toilet.

We moved into another class — or band, as it was called — every six months as new groups of girls entered. Discipline increased as we were elevated from one band to the next. As we matured in our religious life, each new band brought more penances with it.

In the beginning, we had to accuse ourselves after meals. Catholics accept that we are all sinners and are obligated to spend time confessing those sins. At the end of each meal, we would proceed to the head of the table, kneel at the feet of the mistress, and accuse ourselves of whatever infraction we were guilty of, such as breaking silence on the stairs or lessening our food consumption without permission.

The penances for these infractions varied, at times, depending on the mood of Sister Ignatia, the mistress. Sometimes she dismissed us by commanding, "Sister, say a Hail Mary," to which we would respond, "Thank you, Sister," kiss the floor, and return to our seat. Other times, she would reprimand us before the penance and give us the rosary to say. It was similar to going to confession, except that we had to always kiss the floor before returning to our seat at the table. Another penance was to kneel at the wall during supper. This penance was issued at least once a week. We had to take a plate over to a fellow novice, give her the plate to fill, and silently beg for our supper. When she complied, we returned to the wall to eat our supper on our knees. About once a month, six or seven of us had to lie face down at the entrance to the refectory while the other novices stepped over us as they entered.

Every Tuesday and Friday morning we had to wear a chain on our upper arms. The points on the chain would dig into the flesh as the morning wore on, and the marks were visible when the chain was removed, just before noon prayers. Also on Fridays, we had to bare the upper, back part of our legs and whip them with knotted chords while reciting three Our Fathers and three Hail Marys.

We carried out these penances religiously for the entire duration of our stay, which was divided into three phases: postulates, novices, and, finally, professed. Each group was housed in a separate building, although the buildings were connected. We were never allowed to mix except to pray together in the chapel. If, while passing in corridors, a novice spoke to a professed, or a postulant to a novice, for example, each had to ask a penance for violating this rule.

One of the most humbling experiences was when we had to publicly accuse ourselves in front of the entire novitiate. Every second Saturday evening before meditation, about ten names would be posted, and these were required to undergo this humiliation, acknowledging five or six faults each had committed during the month. Accidentally knocking our rosaries against the bench in chapel was considered to be disrespectful and warranted penance. Other infractions could include being late for chapel, or looking at oneself in the framed pictures of previous Mothers General, an act considered to be vain. We weren't allowed to have or use mirrors, so this behavior was usually simply an effort to see if bonnets were on straight — although, truthfully, there was always a touch of vanity to it; after all, we were young girls. The public ritual of this confession of faults was preceded by a fifteen or twenty minute recitation from Sister Ignatia. As each confession was completed, the accused would then kiss the floor and return to their chairs. When all confessions were finished, the accused would be seated in straight rows facing each other with eyes downcast. What a scary experience this was! There was no set standard for punishment. We never knew how much we would be reprimanded for what we accused ourselves. I was particularly affected, because it brought out feelings of rejection in me stemming back to childhood. I found it difficult to cope with these suppressed anxieties. As a result, I tried to claim culpability that wouldn't bring out anger in Sister Ignatia, giving her little option but to let me escape with, "Kiss the floor, Sister."

We had our own hierarchy and strict guidelines about crossing lines. Seniority brought with it certain advantages, as did prior college training and academic achievement. The rewards could include special charges, such as weilding the electric clipper or manning the electric polisher for the highly waxed floors. Discipline was essential. So was caution, since there were always spies among us — what we referred to as "squeal cats" — who would betray any of us who broke the rules.

I was charged with cleaning the third floor lavatory in the novitiate one day when I discovered from the novice assigned to work with me that my old music teacher, Sister Patricia, was from her hometown of Lowell, Massachusetts. Since nuns were forbidden to talk about their whereabouts, past or present, we never knew anything about any of the Sisters we had in school. I was excited to learn this little piece of Sister Patricia's history and pumped the novice for as much information as I could get from her. She confessed breaking the silence to the novice mistress and, therefore, revealed me as the instigator of the violation. I was punished and threatened with a six month delay in professing my first vows — the equivalent of failure to move ahead a grade in public school.

One afternoon , I was trying to cram for an upcoming biology exam in study hall when I met Sister Christine. Biology was one of my worse subjects. It turned out that this fellow Sister was so proficient in biology that she eventually taught the subject in high school. However, each positive social interaction I experienced seemed to be followed by some sort of negative repercussion. Sister Ignatia accused me of conducting a particular friendship because of that brief encounter. Close liaisons were strictly forbidden as they were considered to make the order unstable. Sister Christine and I ran into each other again days later on the grounds outside and studied while walking together along the garden paths. On these hot summer nights, we were occasionally allowed to study outside. I flunked my exam. The Professor Sister suggested that I needed tutoring and recommended that the Sister excelling most at biology be assigned to work with me. As fate would have it, Sister Christine turned out to be my tutor.

We were also assigned to clean the Professed Sisters' parlors together. This gave me the opportunity to see everyone who came in, including some of our old Sister teachers who dropped by for music lessons on Saturday. I, in turn, reported the comings and goings to those in my recreation group. We were required to recreate in threes to avoid close liaisons with what was termed "particular friendships."

I longed for some deodorant or talc powder. Such worldly luxuries were never permitted. However, we were given foot powder from time to time. We changed stockings twice a week. Wearing black cotton stockings for three days at a time without washing them tended to make some sort of foot deodorizer necessity, so Sister Ignatia accumulated all the foot powder and talc that were intended as gifts from our families and mixed them together in a gallon jug. With special permission, we would obtain and empty a fruit jar and fill it with this concocted powder. It was intended for the feet, but I used it as talc, too.

We wore our everyday habit daily except Sunday, and washed it only every six months. At wash time, we literally took it apart — sleeves out, skirt detached from the waist, collar ripped out — and put it together with the others into one large industrial washing machine. Sisters would be assigned to the sewing room to reassemble them. for another six months. In the meantime, we would be issued a new habit to wear. For us, it was like shopping at Saks Fifth Avenue. Our Sunday habits went through the same process, except they were washed only once a year.

As archaic as these rituals sound, they were all part of the process of removing us from worldly possessions, desires and customs, thus placing us into the mental and physical state of abject poverty. By stripping us of all comforts, it also helped us redirect focus away from ourselves.

I caught a cold and developed a sore throat one morning as my final days of the novitiate approached. A number of the Sisters had been sick during the two years I was there, but this was the first time I had taken ill. I was in Scripture class and my condition worsened as the morning dragged on. Finally, I couldn't tolerate it any longer and went to ask Sister Ignatia for cold capsules and something for my sore throat. I could barely stand up and knew I had a temperature. She made me kneel down and kiss the floor because I hadn't come to see her when she was giving out pills the night before. There were only certain days, at 4:45 p.m., when permissions would be given; this was not one of those days. I felt like I was in a no-win situation; I was damned if I went for cold pills and damned if I didn't. At that point, I was so sick I didn't care.

She sent me to see what the convent calls the Infirmarian (known as the infirmary nurse in most schools), Sister Loretta, who was in the professed house.

"Are you rejecting?" Sister Loretta wanted to know.

"I feel like throwing up," I answered, not quite understanding what she was asking.

"Where is your mistress?" she asked, after taking my temperature. "I want you to move into the novices' infirmary."

I knew at that moment that I was very sick, because she was segregating me from the others. I thought I was going to die.

It was March 15. Sister Ignatia didn't come to check on me until the 18th. She told Sister Loretta that I was just looking for sympathy.

"Then why did you send her to me if she wasn't sick," Sister Loretta exclaimed. "She had a temperature of 104 degrees when she arrived."

This seemed to humble Sister Ignatia and she changed her attitude by inquiring how I felt.

I was in bed for the festivities of St. Patrick and St. Joseph. Feast days in the convent were celebrated with special dinners, favors and recreation at meals. For five days, I was abandoned by all, except Sister Loretta, who checked on me once a day, and the novice who brought my meals but couldn't speak to me.

I performed my field practice once a week in St. Mary's School in Cambridge during the last six months of my training. The Sister Superior reminded me of Sister Ann in that she forced me to eat. As we were approaching the final days of our training, the Provincial asked each of us one night at recreation where we'd like to go.

"Not to a large community," I responded.

The night before my first vows, I was summoned by the Provincial to receive my first assignment. I was being sent to St. Mary's, the only novice to be sent to the school in which she had practice-taught. There were fifty-six Sisters in St. Mary's and I didn't want to be one of them.

Sister Provincial explained, "They need a kindergarten teacher and a second music teacher in that school."

It was settled. My stomach began to knot up just thinking about what I was about to face, especially with having another tyrant as Sister Superior. The eight days spent in solid silence at the annual retreat prior to the transition didn't help much in settling my frayed nerves and frazzled constitution.

Vow Day was held in a private morning ceremony with the bishop in attendance. The music provided by the voices of 121 nuns was truly magnificent. A spiritual awareness permeated my entire body and soul as I proclaimed my first vows:

"I, Sister Marie Timothy, solemnly vow and promise to you, your Majesty, and to you, Sister Provincial, the vows of poverty-chastity and obedience for one year."

Three in our group were held back from vows — one because of illness and two because of having a particular friendship, which was considered a serious infraction never to be tolerated.

We received the black veil that established us as full pledged Sisters of Notre Dame and were treated to a five-course breakfast with recreation. Our entire families were allowed to visit later that afternoon. Mother was thrilled beyond words. Dad arrived later. He always drove up alone each month and never interacted with Mum. He just sort of sat on the outside circle staring at me. This day was no different. I often wondered what he was thinking about, but never had the opportunity to try to find out.

The following morning, we moved into the professed house, where we remained from February to August to prepare for the grade we were assigned to teach.

On August 4, 1954, we departed for our prescribed destinations. This was the first time we had been separated in three years.

Monsignor Gleason gave a picnic for us each summer during our training. These were held on the Gloucester property left to one of the Sisters, but our "graduation" picnic was at Beverly Farms on the ocean. Mum did all the buying and cooking — nothing was spared. Well, except alcohol. A highlight was when Aunt Nell arrived in her Jeep, accompanied by her parrot companion. She drove the nuns, decked out in full habit, around the Gloucester harbor, the parrot squawking away at passersby. It was like seeing a flock of out-of-place birds on the beach — penguins in the tropics in July. What laughs she provided! Aunt Nell was always a hit. The Sisters adored her, especially her choice of vocabulary. Nell was definitely colorful in the use of the English language. It was appropriate that she had a parrot for a pet — she could out-swear any sailor, including Blackbeard himself.

Pictures of that sight would have been great, but they were another taboo. It was the 1950s. Nuns were not allowed to pose or have photographs taken of them. Still, it would have made a perfect keepsake to mark the end of one period in my life and the beginning of another. The cocoon was about to hatch.

Photo History

The Early Years

Dad and me — after blizzard in Beverly Farms, 1944

Age 4, solo tapping, 1938

Nana Caughlin, circa 1945.

Confirmation sixth grade, 1946

Age 5, tap dancing class, 1939

Uncle John and me the night before leaving for convent, 1951

High school graduation, 1951

Aunt Nell and me the day of entrance, 1951.

Waltham entrance day, with Dad, 1951

Entrance day with Mum, 1951

Just capped on entrance day with Marie C. and Mary W., 1951

Homestead, Beverly Farms, Mass., circa 1985. The house appeared in the movie "Paper Moon."

Mum, silver-hair legislator for Massachusetts, 1985

Mum being honored as 1994 Senior of the Year, Massachusetts

The Convent

St. Thomas, Peabody, Massachusetts, 1954. Just made final vows.

1959 - final vows.

1966 - modified habit.

Jubilee at Beverly Farms, 1954,
(L-R) Father DeAddar, me, Msgr.
Gleason and Sister Mary Madden.

St. Mary's, Cambridge, 1954. First
assignment.

First time home in 14 years,
for three hours, 1965.
(L-R) Aunt Nell (partially missing),
Billy Maciel, Uncle Murph, Aunt Ann,
me, Dad, Cousin Jack and Mum.

Waltham visiting day. Mum and me, 1951.

Me and Mum in Cambridge, 1955.

East Boston, ABCD, 1963.

Exeter, New Hampshire. Kevin King, Sister Paulina, me, Sister Marie Gabriel accepting keys to a new car, 1963.

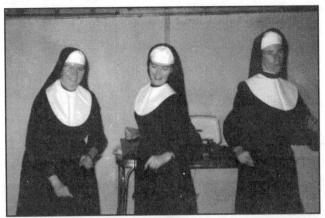

Clowning around in Exeter, New Hampshire, 1964.
Sister Francis, me and Sister Paulina,

Tea at new convent wing dedication, 1969.
Sister Alice, Sister Paulina and me. Exeter, New Hampshire.

Exeter, New Hampshire, 1965.
Mum, Aunt Liza, me, Aunt Nell, Uncle
Murph and Aunt Ann.

Mum, me and Dad, 1967.

Post Convent - Family Life

Sherburne principal, 1988. Checking thermometer for money collected for new playground.

TOP: Chairing JFK ball at The Breakers, Palm Beach, Florida, 1993.
(L-R) Bob Hogan, Colie, me, Brian Hogan, Vivianne Hogan, Sharon Hogan, Kim Hogan and Jim Hogan.

Principal preparing for assembly, 1997.

Principal, 1984-1989.

Sister Jon Julie and me, 1998. One-hundred fiftith dedication of SND. Boston.

Leaving Exeter as Sister Marie. Awarded 1971.

Boston Harbour Cruise, 1998. Me and Sister Christine Julie.

Me and Sister Paulina, 1997.

Fiftieth reunion of Sisters I entered with, 2001. Wells, Maine.

Girls night out, Palm Beach, Florida, 1999. (L-R) Mary Hardy, Madelyn Passarella, me, Paula Peterson, Imelda Slomka and Carla Spurlock

Bobby Kennedy, Jr., and me, 2001. Thirty-fifth anniversary of JFK Medical Center. Atlantis, Florida.

Me and Miss America Shawntel Smith, 1996. Palm Beach, Florida.

New Hampshire Teachers attending my 65th birthday party at Four Seasons, Palm Beach, 1999. Muriel Ward, Myrt Moore, Penny Bodwell, Barbara Doyle and me.

LEFT: Enroute to fashion show. Rye Beach, New Hampshire, 1995. Beryl Lucey, me and Maureen Oleinik.

JFK Medical Center Volunteer Week, 2001. Jeanie Teresé and me.

Colie and me, marriage, 1989.

Colie's 80th birthday, 1997. Ten Hogan stepchildren: Tom, Jim, Mary, Ed, Ann Marie, Kevin, Alice, Paul, Bob and Brian.

My 65th at Four Seasons, Palm Beach, 1999. Colie, me, Carol and Bill Maciel.

Cape Cod, 1990

Colie and me, 1992. North Conway, New Hampshire.

Thanksgiving, 1989. Atlantis, Florida.

Me and Colie, 1991. Bob Hogan's wedding.

Shopping in Delray, Florida, 2001. Emily, Molly, me, and Kim Hogan.

Granddaughter Mary Ann's Engagement Party. Ritz,
Palm Beach. The late Mary Ann, me and Colie.

Bob Hogan and me, 1997,
clowning around. Florida.

Ann Marie, me and Vivianne arriving at Mar-a-Lago
Palm Beach for a fashion show, 1997.

Mrs. America Pageant. Worster, Massachusetts, 1995. Deidre Hogan, Marcia Hogan, Maureen Oleinik, me, Vivianne Hogan., Kim Hogan, and Ann Marie Evans.

Exeter. Me, James and Brian Toye. Picnic before moving to North Carolina, 1990.

Me and Brian Hogan, kitchen buddies at Thanksgiving, 1999.

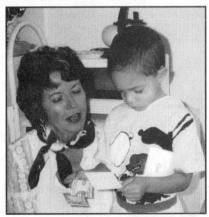

Me and Ryan Hogan, 1999. Learning to read.

Shopping with Deb Hogan, Palm Beach, Florida, 2000.

Snuggling with Adrienne and Claire Hogan, 1999.

Me and Mike Hogan, 1991.

Mary Toye, me, Cynthia Hogan and Alice Hogan, 1991.

Me and Liz Hogan, Exeter, New Hampshire,1998.

Pat Hogan, Boston, 1999

Exeter, New Hampshire, 1998. James Toye, Timmy Hogan and Margaret Hogan.

Tony and Teri Maciel, 1999. New Hampshire.

First home as Mrs Hogan, Amesbury, Massachusetts, 1989.

First home built in Rye Beach, New Hampshire, 1983

Atlantis home, 2002.

Exeter home sundeck, 1993.

Exeter home backyard, 1993.

The Modeling Years

Graduation from modeling school, 1990.

Modeling, 1992

Cape Cod, 1993

Ipswich River, 2001

Three awards: Mrs Congeniality, Community Service, finalist (one of five), 1995

Headshot, 1991.

Modeling, 1992.

Modeling, 1991

Boston, North End, 1992

Teaching

My first assignment was joining fifty-six other Sisters in teaching at the local parish grammar and high school in Cambridge. We also housed ten Sisters from a nearby neighborhood with a school but no convent, at least not until the late '50s. It was August of 1954 and I was nineteen, one of the youngest in a convent of nuns ranging in age from 19 to 84.

I was immediately introduced to Sister Theresé, the music teacher, and was assigned as her assistant.

Daily disciplines were a little more relaxed now that we were in schools. We could speak during the day, although there were still certain rooms in the convent in which talking was never permitted and we continued having specified recreation time as before. Prayer life was the same.

My assignment was to teach kindergarten, with a daily schedule of five-year-olds divided into two sessions: sixty-four boys in the morning and sixty-four girls in the afternoon. The sexes were segregated; that was a general policy of parochial schools in the mid-20th century.

The local pastor was Monsignor Burke, a kind, gentle soul who dearly loved children. He visited my classroom every morning around 11:15 and stayed on the premises to watch the military dismissal of the entire school at 11:30 for lunch. Rain or snow, the 1200-member student body would assemble in an assigned location in the schoolyard. Marches would play over the intercom outside through strategically placed loud speakers on the church corners so the music could be heard throughout the entire vicinity as the children marched along in silence. The whole student body ritualistically paraded up the street, led by the oldest grades. Marching in unison to the beat of the music, they would proceed to the four corners, where an assigned policeman would then escort them across the busy intersection. The ritual, performed daily at 11:30 a.m. and 3 p.m., from around the community was such a spectacular sight that it regularly attracted onlookers. The Sisters accompanied the students to the corner.

I gave private piano lessons in the convent at the end of the class day every half hour until 5 p.m., when I would then rush to the chapel to get my prayers in before attending community exercises at 6. Professed life was different, but still rugged. After supper, at 7, we had recreation and night prayers as in previous years, but now we also had to work until 9:30 preparing for the next day's class. The preparation took place each night except Saturday or Sunday in a room called St. Ignatius, filled with 56 desks.

My brutal schedule began to take its toll. On Saturday mornings I traveled to Boston University to study violin. I was part of the Archdiocesan Sisters Orchestra that played for several years and was also part of a choral group that practiced certain months of the year. After three years of teaching 128 students a day, tutoring twelve private piano pupils, studying violin, practicing and performing, I began to feel exhausted, weak and extremely dizzy.

Every three years a new Superior was reappointed or transferred unannounced. Just as my health was beginning to fail, we were assigned a new Superior. Sister Rita was a kind, warm, loving and highly spiritual woman who was so gentle that she spoke with a voice like an angel's breath on butterfly wings.

She was concerned about my deteriorating health and had me escorted by a companion Sister to the local doctor. Tests showed my blood count was so low that he was surprised I was able to function. I was given a raw liver injection and was told to come back for monitoring every other day for several months. He requested of Sister Rita that all of my extra activities be canceled until my health was back to normal. For six months my duties excluded violin classes, piano lessons and choral practices. That was enough time for my body to recuperate, and my health started to improve. I was soon back to teaching my regular, full schedule.

Sister Theresé staged Broadway musicals at the school. She'd been a dancing teacher before entering the convent, so these productions were always extravagant. They were held annually as a source of income for the parish. Sister Theresé encouraged me to share her responsibility and I became involved with the program. I loved the dancing activity, as it brought back fond memories of my early teen years when, on Saturday nights, I took ballroom dance lessons that Aunt Eliza paid for at Miss James School of Dancing in Beverly. At my monthly visits in Cambridge, I began to see some of my old classmates from high school and learned that Bobby D had a new romance. He had come to realize that I had settled more into religious life and he would have to forge his life without me.

During summer school, we were either assigned to teach remedial reading and math, even though we did not have degrees (our teaching certificates allowed us to teach in the classroom), or asked to cook in some small convent. Those not needed in the classroom or the kitchen took a course required for obtaining a degree. The process was slow. We wouldn't get our degrees from Emmanuel until 1962 or '63.

After my second year in Cambridge, the Provincial decided to swtich me to teaching first grade. It was felt that I deserved a smaller class as compensation for having carried an extra workload for so long. My student capacity of 64 dropped all the way down to 57.

Wow! What a relief!

I suppose I shouldn't be too sarcastic. After all, the numbers did decrease — though ever so slightly. Truth is, they diminished drastically in time. It was just a slow process. Gradually, the numbers dropped into the 40s and finally down to a total of 25. The burden of teaching was squarely on each teacher's shoulders; we didn't have the luxury of teacher's aides or assistants back then — we were it. Fate would have it that for the next nineteen years, during my entire duration as a nun, I would teach first grade.

After five pleasurable years at St. Mary's Cambridge, I returned to Waltham to prepare for final vows in the summer of 1959, the first time since we had left for our initial assignment in 1954 that my band (class) would all be together.

Monsignor Gleason again sponsored one of his fantastic picnics — and one of his last. Anticipation of Vow Day was high as music practice, favors, and decorating proceeded at an elevated pitch. Rules were somewhat relaxed, so we could invite parents and religious relatives to the morning ceremony. Monsignor was on the altar — proud, but very feeble. After seven years and six months, our training was finally over.

Cardinal Cushing helped the Sisters of Notre Dame buy an estate in Ipswich where he built a $4 million structure to house those Sisters-in-training who eventually would become Sisters of Notre Dame. The old novitiate in Waltham was given to the Marist Sisters. We spent a week during the summer of '59 cleaning the homestead in Ipswich and preparing it for a summer residence for older nuns. The structure would take two years to build.

Later that summer I was transferred to St. Thomas parish in Peabody, Massachusetts — to the delight of Mum and Monsignor Gleason. The mission was only 20 minutes from my home. I've always felt that a personal request from the Monsignor made this transfer possible. He had grown quite feeble and, as an extremely generous benefactor to Notre Dame, had the influence to make such a move feasible. His fondness for me was apparent and open. The immediate proximity of this assignment made it convenient for him to visit.

It was wet, inside and out, the day I left Cambridge — it was raining and I was crying. I arrived at St. Thomas Peabody on August 10, 1959, becoming one of six nuns to serve the affluent community. Of the forty-four first-graders assigned to me, twenty-five of them could already read. Sister Therese's influence was apparent as this parish had an annual musical. and I was given total responsibility for staging the production, and had to make a lot of adjustments. I'd been away from Beverly Farms for seven-and-a-half years and had become quite different from the teenager I'd been when I left. It was somewhat disconcerting to suddenly find myself close to home, wearing a habit, while my mother popped in with goodies on a regular basis. Her constant surprise drop-ins made me apprehensive, because Sister Superior pressured me to keep the visits short. The most difficult adjustment I had to make was not being able to return to my hometown and, therefore, having to contend with only fond memories of the Farms.

It didn't last long though. Another change of Provincials occurred, and the new one made several transfers at the end of her first year in office. I was sent to the farthest mission in the order — Exeter, New Hampshire. It was 98 degrees when I arrived in Exeter on August 13, 1960. The driver who drove me from Peabody left my suitcase on the doorstep. St. Michael's Superior, Sister Ignace, greeted me at the door wearing a long blue work apron and holding a wax cloth in her hand. As one of thirteen nuns who lived in the convent of St. Michael's, I felt as though I'd been delegated to a foreign mission.

Monsignor Gleason was furious with the Provincial about my transfer to Exeter. He let his dissatisfaction be known, to no avail. Exactly thirty days after my arrival in New Hampshire, he succumbed to his earthly frailties and quietly drifted away to join his Maker.

September 12, 1960, was one of the saddest days of my life. I lost a friend and a father figure on that day. He was laid to rest in his family plot in Waltham, an hour or so drive from St. Margaret's, where the High Mass was held in Beverly Farms. We were never allowed to attend funerals or wakes, but I was given special permission to attend his service. I felt so alone. I was among the few nuns from his parish who were there. Sister Ann, my first-grade teacher, was now the local Superior in Beverly Farms. She sneaked me into the rectory to visit my old home and hurried me out so no one would see me. I returned to St. Michael's Exeter that night completely devastated. My faith was intact, but my hope was waning. I was on the verge of despair.

It didn't help that Sister Ignace, the Superior, was cold and distant — completely unsympathetic to my feelings. Not once did she try to understand what I was going through or attempt to reach out and comfort me. This was a trying year for me. I lost one of the most important people in my life and had to contend with one of the worst internal conditions since joining the convent, and I felt that after ten years our training period should be over. I loved every minute of teaching and the people in Exeter became good friends, but my enthusiasm for the Sisterhood was diminishing. Sister Ignace wasn't making it any easier. About the only thing keeping my hope alive that year was the election of a Catholic as President of the United States for the first time in history. Furthermore, John F. Kennedy was from my home state of Massachusetts.

Sister Catherine was one of the young Sisters who taught second grade. She developed a case of laryngitis and, for some reason, Sister Irene, the infirmarian, didn't provide much care for her condition. After three days of watching her suffer, I offered to serve her some egg white and lemon after night prayer while I was in the kitchen preparing for my cooking day.

One of the rituals we had to endure was the "great silence." No one was allowed to speak following night prayer until after breakfast the next day. The stillness created an almost vacuum-like ambience, through which the slightest sound could be heard. Sister Superior heard the eggbeater and came storming into the kitchen.

"What are you doing Sister?" she demanded to know.

"I'm preparing a concoction of egg white and lemon for Sister Catherine," I sheepishly admitted, "to help ease her sore throat."

"How dare you?"

"I'm just trying to help her," I whimpered. "I didn't mean ..."

"Since when did you become the infirmarian?" she admonished sternly. "Throw it out!"

I was stunned.

"Now!" she commanded.

I did as I was instructed and was so shaken by the confrontation that I couldn't even finish preparing the next night's supper. Later that night I slipped a note under Sister Catherine's door explaining what had happened and apologizing for not being able to provide her some relief.

During school recess the next day, Sister Superior summoned me.

"Since you have so aptly demonstrated your concern for the health of your fellow Sisters," she began, "I see no reason why you should not assume the duties officially."

"I didn't mean any harm, Sister Superior," I tried to explain. "I was just trying to help out. I felt bad for Sister Catherine trying so hard to teach those little kids without a voice. It's not like teaching older students who can read a book and keep themselves busy with blackboard assignments. You need your voice for the little ones."

My efforts were falling on deaf ears.

"Still, you want to be a health provider, I see no reason why you shouldn't get your wish," she said. "You are hereby the reigning infirmarian."

I didn't know what to say. I was dumbfounded. I just stood there staring at her with my mouth open without uttering another word. I kept this new, unexpected, extra charge for the next eight years.

On another occasion, Sister Teresa was preparing Sunday dinner and we were in chapel, when suddenly we heard a blood-curdling scream from the kitchen. I ran to see what was going on. Sister Teresa had burned her fingers on a kettle of steam. I brought her upstairs to the medicine closet, applied a salve and was looking for gauze with which to wrap her wound, when Sister Superior walked in.

"What happened here?" she wanted to know.

"Sister Teresa accidentally burned herself while preparing dinner," I explained. "I treated her with some salve and was trying to find something to bandage it with when you came in."

"I think there's some gauze in the school office," she replied, and left.

I decided that, rather than walking across the complex to school, I would not cover Sister Teresa's fingers and would just let them air out. I then took over the dinner preparation while she replaced me in the chapel.

Three days later I received another summons from Sister Superior. I was immediately instructed to kneel down before her as she proceeded to read me the riot act for fifteen minutes.

"You are the most disobedient religious I've lived with in twenty-five years," she concluded.

"I don't understand what you mean," I stuttered, stunned. "Sister Superior, tell me what I've done wrong."

"You know very well what you've done," she continued. "You have failed to follow Article 15 of our rule!".

Article 15 states that we are required to be completely obedient by following "even the wish" of the Superior.

"How did I violate the rule?" I honestly wanted to know.

"You did not go to the school to obtain a gauze for Sister Teresa's burns after I told you that you could find it there."

"I ... I ... didn't realize you were instructing me to go look for it. I thought you were merely suggesting that one might be there if I needed it. I ... I decided that I didn't need it after all."

"Your disobedience will not be tolerated!" she firmly stated. "You should have followed my wishes."

When the new Provincial came for her annual visitation, I summoned enough courage to approach her and confess my concerns that Sister Ignace was way off-balance. I told her about these incidents and even disclosed that the Sister ignored the Provincial's earlier directive to allow us a hot drink while planning schoolwork at night. It was freezing in this convent and the Sisters really needed it.

After the Provincial left, some changes were made. We were provided a hot drink every night, but I was branded from that time forward. Hell came to roost in the convent — for me, anyway.

The medicine closet was locked and I had to ask for the key each time I wanted something for a sick Sister. Nana always said that hot water, sugar and whiskey would get rid of any cold or sore throat, so I adopted this formula for the Sisters. I provided the nuns with hot toddies at night as both a preventive measure and to sooth any oncoming colds. When Sister Ignace got wind of it, she began to keep track of the whiskey bottles. Getting rid of the empties and replacing them without notice was an ongoing dilemma that soon became a running joke in my family. I would persuade Mum to take the empty bottles with her on visiting days. The running gag was that she and my aunts would guess how many she'd have to chuck in the dumpster at the nearby state park on a given trip — four or five? Even Dad got pulled into the operation. He visited on Sundays when the family wasn't there, and would bring an occasional bottle of whiskey — but not without inquiring about what was happening with them. When I'd tell him about Mum taking the empties, he'd be astonished at how much was consumed. I found myself on the defensive, explaining that thirteen of us lived there and if one got sick, sometimes three or four might follow.

Sister Ignace's two-year tenure ended. Sister Paulina replaced her. What a drastic change! Sister Paulina was a warm, wonderful woman who was far ahead of her time. She displayed acts of kindness with a liberal attitude and remarkable compassion. If there was a reason to celebrate during the week, she allowed us to watch Lawrence Welk on television. The pastor in Exeter had a cottage at Seabrook Beach. We had to pray and keep silence all day on the first Sunday of each month. She allowed us to walk the beach in full habit in the fall and winter, and go into the pastor's cottage for a hot cup of tea, then pray at the beach. Her liberal actions were regularly reported and she underwent constant scrutiny, plus firm chastisements on every yearly visit from the Provincial. We were not allowed to be publicly involved in any social activity, so she arranged with the local theater owner to have private showings for the Sisters in the area.

She was severely reprimanded for organizing a private screening of "Dr. Zhivago." So much pressure was brought to bear on Sister Paulina that after her fifth year as Superior of Exeter, she could take no more and resigned her post.

Significant changes were taking place in the Catholic Church. The Second Vatican Ecumenical Council convened under the auspices of Pope John XXIII in 1962. Pope John's desire was for the Council to "increase the fervour and energy of Catholics" and "to serve the needs of Christian people." The Council outlined a number of objectives in order to achieve that goal. Bishops and priests had to escalate in holiness; the laity had to be provided effective instruction in the Christian faith; schooling in morals was needed; Christian social activity had to increase; adequate education of children had to be provided; and Christians had to develop missionary hearts. Pope John sought to bring the Church up to date. He wanted it to adapt itself to meet the challenges of modern times. He conveyed his message succinctly when someone probed him on the subject. Like most Italians, he loved expressive gestures and had a flair for the dramatic. When asked to reveal his intentions, he simply moved to a window and threw it open to let in a draft of fresh air.

His successor in 1963 was Paul VI, the pontiff most associated with the Council. It would be his responsibility at its conclusion to implement the decrees of Vatican II. Pope Paul VI was a popular religious leader who was determined to reach out to Christians and non-Christians alike in working toward world peace. He was adamant about holding firmly to basic Catholic teachings on faith and morals, and showed an open willingness to do whatever was necessary to bring the Catholic Church out of the Dark Ages and into the Twentieth Century.

We were beginning to feel the vibrations of those changes all the way over here on the other side of the globe.

Our new Superior, Sister Alice, continued the techniques and practices of her predecessor. She, too, had a liberal approach, which some felt went beyond the intentions of Vatican II. The Council closed in 1965, and by then, a number of changes had already begun to take place. The rules at the convent had become more lenient. We were allowed to shorten our habit and let our hair grow so that, with a modified veil, the hair would show. The silence rules were relaxed and we could talk at daily meals. Less-stringent attitudes prevailed. I had not been home in fourteen years. We were now allowed to go home for a day once a year (later it was changed to three days) and watch educational TV. Thanks to Sisters Paulina and Alice, even those privileges were stretched in such ways as expanding the definition of "educational" television programming. I always dreamed of someday meeting Lawrence Welk so I could tell him that his show was my salvation in the '60s. For us nuns, it was educational.

Mum had kept my driver's license current by using my home address, so I was able to drive again. Perhaps the most significant impact Vatican II had on my life was allowing me to reconnect with the outside world. I began to get involved with public education. While the bells of St. Michael's rang at Exeter, the chimes of St. Julie's spirit resounded in my heart. I was ready to stand up for my convictions.

Community Involvement

Some six-year-olds in New Hampshire were not developmentally ready to enter school in the 1960s. This problem grew with each of the eleven years I taught in Exeter. I'm not sure what caused the trend, because it hadn't seemed a big issue in previous decades, when children were adequately prepared by their parents for entrance into public and parochial schools. I knew that I had been ready, but that was no longer the case with first-graders. I suspect it was related to the changes of the time. Upheavals throughout the social structure were occurring in the '60s. Student protests against America's involvement in Vietnam followed racial riots over civil rights. The single-breadwinner family was becoming a thing of the past as rising costs forced both parents to work. Television became the family's primary baby-sitter. For whatever reason, the needs of children were being neglected at an alarming rate. I could see the growth of its impact at the beginning of each school term.

As part of its attempt to address this problem, The League of Women Voters asked me in 1969 to sign a petition for mandatory kindergarten in Exeter. Expressing my concerns, I had established a reputation in the community, and the League believed that if they could persuade me to support their efforts, the parishioners at St. Michael's would soon follow and add 500 supporters to their cause. Their efforts may have been based on sound logic, but there was one slight predicament. I didn't believe what they were proposing was the answer to the problem. I preferred that transition or readiness classes be made available to six-year-olds who were not ready to attend school, as required by law. I seized the opportunity provided by the League to crusade for this method, which I thought was the solution.

My campaign gained enough recognition that eventually Dr. Adamo, the local superintendent of schools, asked to meet with me. Since I was prohibited from going to his office, he met with me at the convent to discuss my idea. He invited me to an executive session of the school board, and my Provincial granted special permission for me to attend. A blue ribbon committee was formed to investigate. I was assigned to serve on this committee. We studied the number of retentions in first grade, reading scores and other factors. As a result of these studies and on the recommendation of our committee, two transition classes were formed the following year, and the program continued from that time forth. To this day, Exeter has a program of transition or readiness classes.

The effect of Vatican II was gradually being felt. The rules in the convent became increasingly flexible. We could eat in public. We were able to get more involved with the community and its politics. We were even given a stipend of $15 a month to be used for necessities, such as telephone calls, cosmetics, personal items, and clothing.

My community involvement brought another crusade to my doorstep. Working closely with Ginny Holder, the public school nurse, I found myself campaigning to rectify issues surrounding learning disabilities. Together, we became state directors of the New Hampshire Association for Children with Learning Disabilities. I also became involved with the national organization, ACLD, as I became increasingly dedicated to the needs of learning disabled kids.

Several of the local parishioners approached me to run for the Exeter School Board. A religious had never, to my knowledge, held an elected office before, at least not in this part of New England. I prayed long hours diligently for guidance. Finally, I decided to petition the Provincial and her advisory board for permission to pursue a seat on the panel. They discussed and debated the issue for three months, then asked me to prepare a position paper and report back. Much to my surprise, it was accepted and I was given the green light. The decision was announced to the province of 1200 nuns and they were supportive. Part of my platform was that Christian living and giving extended beyond the church, and that contributing to those outside our walls was the message from Vatican II that had been in vogue for several years.

The Provincial encouraged me to discuss the matter with the New Hampshire bishop. Although Bishop Primeau had no jurisdiction over us, as we were a papal order, it would be a courteous gesture and certainly would not hurt to have his blessing. Sister Alice, as St. Michael's Sister Superior, and I made a trip to Manchester to be interviewed by the bishop. We were not prepared for the resistance we received. Apparently, our local pastor had notified the bishop in advance of our arrival and had prejudiced him against the idea. What was intended strictly as a courtesy call caused a monumental clash. Now we faced a major dilemma by having the approval of the order complicated by the disapproval of the bishop on the state level.

"It is against Canon Law for a religious to participate," Bishop Primeau said, "and, furthermore, you'll be a national figure."

This changed everything. Although the road with the order had been a long one, the fight was just beginning. The bishop's disapproval caused widespread apprehension among my supporters — especially with my financial backers, Bud Dunfey from Dunfey Corp. and Colie Hogan from McCord Corp. They were as let down as I was. I had to decide whether to continue. I knew this meant that the controversy inherent in the fight would escalate. Deep in my heart, I felt I could win, but I couldn't help wondering what price would have to be paid in the long run. If harmony were absent inside the camp, how in the world could I expect it on the outside? And what kind of damage would be done to the religious order in the final analysis if I pursued the struggle? It wasn't worth it. I withdrew my nomination. The nuns who had rallied behind me were stunned.

I was appointed first counselor to the superior. In layman terms, it was like serving as an assistant principal. I continued to teach first-graders having a class of 40. Plus, I was involved with the parish's 50-member choir. I also continued my involvement with local and state politics, and couldn't help myself when it came to getting involved, especially with my favorite crusade — learning disabled children.

Head Start is a child development program for children from low-income families, one of the many outstanding social programs created by Sargent Shriver in the 1960s. In Boston, Head Start operated under the auspices of an agency called Action for Boston Community Development. I was asked to become the agency's Head Start director one summer. I became the only religious in the state to head the program, opening the door to unimaginable mayhem, for which I was totally unprepared.

I was accustomed to dealing with children who were reasonably disciplined and, as a result, tended to take certain things for granted. For example, most children were conditioned to respond to the bell ringing as a signal to prepare for the next phase of their class; or get in line to go to lunch, go to recess, go back to class, and so forth. The inner-city kids in the Head Start program reacted to the bell as though the gates at the racetrack had opened. Ring! And they're off! We might as well have announced over the intercom, "Let's get ready to rummmble!!!" because they just went berserk, scattering in all directions.

Picture this: an overgrown penguin racing down the streets of East Boston chasing after a miniature hoodlum. It was quite a footrace, but there I was, sprinting down the sidewalk with my skirt and hood flapping in the wind. I must have been a sight to behold during those first few weeks, running in all directions, climbing fire escapes, darting in and out of buildings, trying to drag these little bolts of energy back to class.

I started to get an idea of who these kids were, and why they were so different from the others I was used to, when I met the parents or guardians. We weren't allowed to make home visits, so they had to come to us at the convent. I soon learned how dysfunctional the environment was for these children. It was not unusual for them to come from a single parent home or even be raised by another relative. Fathers, more often than not, had either fled the scene or were in prison. There was no discipline, no rules, no structure, and no responsibility.

The defining moment for me in understanding the psychology of these youngsters came when we took them to Massachusetts General Hospital for routine checkups. They freaked out approaching the building and went ballistic at the sight of the nurses and doctors. It was as if they had witnessed or experienced some sort of traumatic event involving health care providers that caused them to react demonstratively at what most children view as routine. Forget the needles — the outfits were enough to set them off. They responded overtly to authority figures in general — in fact, to anyone in a uniform, including us nuns.

These children were a definite challenge and it was difficult for both them and me to adjust. In time, somewhat of a routine was established and, I like to think, I had an impact on these young lives.

My cousin, Bill Maciel, came to visit me in the convent while I was working with the Head Start program. He had visited on a number of occasions dating back to my early years as a postulate when he was so small that he wasn't even included in the maximum count for visitors. Bill was a sweet kid who had grown into an exceptional young man. This time he sought my advice. He wanted to get engaged to his girlfriend, Carol, and asked how I thought the family would react. Regardless how others responded, I assured him that he had my blessings. I only regretted that I couldn't attend the wedding.

The state ACLD offered me a grant to further my studies in the field of learning disabilities at any place in the country I preferred during the summer of 1969. I chose to attend American International College in Springfield, Massachusetts. AIC had an operating student clinic as well as a fine program on teaching children with learning disabilities. Sixteen years of teaching first grade helped me tremendously to achieve excellent grades in all the courses. The reading supervisor, Sister Helen, persistently encouraged me to work toward a masters degree. I had never thought it was important enough to pursue. Although I did give it some serious thought the year after completing the courses at AIC, my feeling was that a masters degree was just a status symbol and I could continue doing a fine job without it. I was also offered a Montessori Fellowship at Boston College, which I declined.

More and more Sisters were getting involved in various ministries or apostolates. I was beginning to think about coming out of the classroom myself, but, being in a teaching order, what would I do?

Many of the young Sisters were becoming disenchanted with religious life and felt it wasn't for them.

One day, Sister Kevin came and told me she wanted to leave, and asked how to do it.

For some years, priests from a nearby religious order were our confessors. I telephoned to ask for their guidance.

"Hello," answered a warm, gentle voice.

"Hello, this is Sister Marie Timothy at St. Michael's. Could I speak with someone about counseling for one of our young Sisters."

"This is Father Liam. I can help you."

Father Liam was Father Superior of the order, a kind-hearted, peaceful, loving holy man — the perfect type of person to serve as a father confessor.

"Could you suggest someone to talk to Sister Kevin, who is contemplating leaving the convent after four years?" I asked.

"I'd be glad to see her," he said. "Could you bring her over here at 5 o'clock"

"We'll be there," I answered.

We Sisters were required to sign out the car each time one of us wanted to use it, and state where we were going. I don't recall exactly how I made the log entry, but I do remember that I was coy with regard to Sister Kevin. I tried to keep her intention quiet, as leaving the order was becoming a trend and I didn't want to fuel the migration.

It was a fifteen-minute ride to the ocean. As we entered the monastery, a handsome and charming priest greeted us.

"I'm Father Liam," he introduced himself.

"Hi, I'm Sister Marie Timothy and this is Sister Kevin."

"My pleasure," he said, then excused himself and left me sitting in the foyer as he and Sister Kevin disappeared into the parlor to talk. Some fifteen minutes later, they emerged and he stunned me by saying, "Sister Marie

Timothy — that's a pretty name." I was amazed that he remembered my name after such a brief encounter.

He continued to counsel Sister Kevin for the next three months until she peacefully and quietly left the order. About the same time, another Sister discovered that her parents had started drinking heavily and become alcoholics while she was in the convent. Since she had not been able to return home for years, she hadn't realized this problem had developed. She needed counseling to adjust. Once again, Father Liam responded. I found myself turning to him more and more as problems with the Sisters came up. This was another of the effects of Vatican II. In the past, we had no alternative but to go to the Superior with whatever problems or situations we faced. Now the tide was changing and with it came the freedom to reach out and consult with anyone we desired.

Father Liam gave holy hours in different convents. He was a joy to listen to and an inspiration to Sisters and laity alike seeking to persevere.

By 1970, I had served an unprecedented ten years in Exeter, each year fearing it would be my last at St. Michael's. I found myself asking the Provincial each year if she planned to transfer me, because I didn't want to accept a reappointment to the State ACLD board if I couldn't fulfill the requirements. She always assured me that I would be staying in Exeter for at least another year, stating explicitly that I was doing great work in New Hampshire and particularly in Exeter. That pretty much guaranteed that the order had no intention of sending me elsewhere.

The Sisters of Notre Dame were still struggling to overcome a bad impression that had been attached to the order for almost eighteen years. My high-profile activity and efforts were helping to overcome the sizable image problem we suffered in the community.

The institution's reputation began souring in 1950, the year before I took my first vows and long before I was assigned to the area. Bishop Brady, the local diocesan bishop, wanted the Sisters of Notre Dame in his diocese in New Hampshire. He had jurisdiction over the Mercy Sisters then serving in St. Michael's parish. He ordered them out to make room for the Sisters of Notre Dame, the transition occurring practically overnight. The local populace was devastated by the upheaval and sudden transformation. There was a drastic mood change in Exeter and residents began referring to the new arrivals as "the black witches."

The Sisters of Mercy were not a cloistered order and, as such, had been administering to the sick, visiting the lonely and interacting with the people of the parish on a regular basis. They were interconnected with the community. The Sisters of Notre Dame, on the other hand, was a semi-cloistered order and its nuns could not visit the sick, grocery shop or ever leave the convent except to go to the hospital for treatment, attend school, attend church or respond to an emergency. We were so bound to the convent that we even had to have our groceries delivered, and doctors had to make house calls. As a result, we were much more isolated from the community than the order we superseded.

After eighteen years, we were still slow to gain the community's support. In the late '60s, however, it was beginning to happen . The progressiveness of the Church as it followed the Spirit of Vatican II was finally reaching the small town of Exeter, New Hampshire. The community that once referred to us as "the black witches" was gradually coming to accept us as productive assets. The more we interrelated with the people, the more they came to accept us. I felt as though my efforts were an integral part of that change.

I was convinced that my Superior at St. Michael's and those throughout the order shared that conviction. That's why I was flabbergasted when a letter arrived on August 1, 1970, informing us that I and four other Sisters were being transferred.

I was reassigned to Weymouth, Massachusetts. My obedience prevailed. Accepting my obligation, I made telephone calls to parishioners, state officials, local school officials and various religious advisors to inform them of my transfer and to bid them good-bye. I had only three days to pack and leave.

On the morning of the day I was to leave I received a telephone call from the Provincial.

"I've been inundated with calls," Sister Provincial said.

As the Provincial, she was the first to receive reactions to my transfer. And the reactions came in abundance from all levels of government and walks of life.

"I don't have any choice," she continued. "We didn't expect this kind of reaction. Therefore, we will have to keep you in Exeter for the time being. Your transfer is being terminated, but let me make it perfectly clear that this will only be for one year."

"I understand, Sister," I responded. "I hope you don't think I had anything to do with this. I assure you that I had nothing to do with those phone calls."

"I know that, Sister. I never thought otherwise. It's just that under the circumstances, this seems to be the best way to handle the situation."

My thorough dedication to the cause of helping learning disabled children, coupled with a daunting schedule, had produced burnout. I was exhausted, and by 1971, working in the classroom no longer had the appeal that it had in the beginning. I didn't want to leave Notre Dame — but what would I do?

The summer of that year brought about more unexpected changes. First, our great Superior, Sister Alice, was pulled from us unannounced. We had a difficult time getting an appointment to see the Provincial to protest her departure and, when we finally did, she told us it was a conscience matter, which meant it wasn't open for discussion. Case closed.

Our assignments were made in early June. I was to be sent to a parish in Cambridge, Massachusetts, not far from where I started teaching in 1954. My respondibility was to teach a half-year while simultaneously training two young student Sisters from Emmanuel College. In mid-year I was to return to Wheelock College full-time to finish my masters. I would remain at the convent in Cambridge and commute the short distance to the college on Massachusetts Bay Transit Authority vehicles.

The new Superior in Cambridge, Sister Agnes, was the female equivalent of Attila the Hun. She was the toughest Superior I had known up to that point. I felt like I was being catapulted back into the Dark Ages.

The humiliation started almost immediately. I got up to leave at the end of my first community supper, and was both astonished and embarrassed when she sent me back to wait for the rest of the Sisters to finish their meal. I had come from an environment in which we simply left the table after eating to attend to our many commitments. At the other convents where I'd stayed, long mess tables were used for meals. Here, tables around the refectory were small, and no one left their seat until everyone had finished eating. I was mortified at the spectacle she made of me in front of the others, especially the younger Sisters.

Within the first few days at the Blessed Sacrament Convent, I developed an agonizing sensation of regressing — not just to an earlier period in my own life, but into an earlier century. It was like living in medieval times. I was thirty-eight years old and found myself treated as though I were a spoiled five-year-old.

The pastor, Monsignor Bukay, on the other hand, was very friendly and welcomed me warmly when I went to my classroom prior to school opening.

"I understand you came to us from Exeter," he said.

"Yes, Monsignor," I replied.

"Having to make a move after eleven years in one place can be quite traumatic. What can I do to help make the transition more pleasant? Is there any way I can make your stay here happier?"

By now, I was teaching creatively. I had developed techniques that made the room here difficult to work in.

"Well," I said, "it would help if the desks and chairs nailed to the classroom floor were removed. And perhaps you could purchase a rug to help muffle the noise and make the room a little cozier."

"I'll take care of it," he said, and to my surprise he fulfilled his promise within a week.

Making such a request to the Monsignor may not have been the most politically correct thing for me to do, given the fact that the Sister Superior had immediately demonstrated her contempt for me. And, as one might expect, I dearly paid for the oversight .

I was in the classroom the day before school opened when a working father, on his lunch hour, came with his six-year-old son to be tested before entering first grade. This caught me unprepared. I was totally ignorant of the procedure at Blessed Sacrament School and asked for his patience while I sought help. The door to Sister Superior's office was open and I could see the Monsignor talking to her, so I waited patiently for them to finish their conversation. After twenty or thirty minutes, I began to feel uneasy about inconveniencing the man waiting patiently in my classroom. I gently knocked on the door.

"Excuse me, Sister, Monsignor, for interrupting you, but there's a father on his lunch hour in my classroom with his son. He wants to have the child tested and registered for first grade and I'm not ..."

Pointing her finger at me as though I were a five-year-old, she reprimanded, "Can't you see I'm busy with Monsignor? How rude. Leave this office at once!"

I was too humiliated to even go back in the classroom to face the waiting man. I broke into tears and rushed to the convent full of embarrassment, devastated with feelings of rejection. I have no idea what happened to the father and his son. They were gone by the time I returned to the classroom. Later that afternoon, I was surprised when I looked up and saw the Monsignor enter, his face filled with genuine concern.

"I just thought I'd drop by and see if you were okay," he said. "That was a rather harsh reaction on the part of Sister Agnes."

"I didn't mean to disturb you or her," I tried to explain. "It's just that I knew the boy's father was running out of time. He had to get back to work. I was just trying to get help."

"I know," he said, consolingly. "Sister Agnes can be quite demonstrative at times, but that outburst was unusual even for her. She seems to have a particular interest in you. You arrived with an excellent reputation from your work in Exeter and you come with exceptional credentials. I think there may be a touch of jealousy involved here. Is there anything I can do to ease the situation?"

"I appreciate that, Monsignor, I really do, but it would probably only make matters worse. This is something I need to handle myself. I know what I need to do — it's just not my style."

"What's that?" he asked.

"I need to get angry instead of so emotional and tell her off."

"Well, just bear in mind that I'm here if you need me."

"Thank you, Monsignor, I appreciate that."

He left. The animosity from Sister Superior continued and I spoke about it with Monsignor Bukay periodically for the next several months. However, it wasn't my nature to confess such innermost feelings to a virtual stranger, and I found myself turning more to my confidant in New Hampshire, Father Liam. We kept in touch on a regular weekly basis discussing these issues in depth. He insisted that I take her to task and put her in her place; otherwise she would just continue the abuse.

His logic made sense, the psychology was accurate, and it probably would work in another world. But this was the convent, and the rules of action were different. Priests could operate more freely. Without the kind of restrictions that we had, they did weren't required to observe obedience to the degree dictated by the convent. Therefore, it wasn't practical for me to act on such advice from a male clergyman. After all, it was in the early days of St. Ignatius when males initiated the tough rules by which our Sisters were forced to live. Things haven't changed much since then. The role of females was viewed as quite different from men in the first century. Women were thought to be subservient and societal constraints were often confining and severe. The sisterhood still operated under those dictates in the 20th century.

The antagonism from Sister Superior increased. It became so bad that, one night in October 1971, I borrowed a neighbor's car and drove to Ipswich to see the Provincial. The sister governing the province had entered the order with me some twenty years ago. I poured out my heart and soul to her.

"You've got to get me out of there, Sister Helen," I pleaded. "If you don't remove me over the Christmas vacation, I'm afraid I'll crack up."

She scheduled her annual Cambridge visitation for later that week. She wanted to survey the situation firsthand

and get an accurate overview by interviewing each Sister individually. The majority of the nuns were content with conditions at the convent and with serving under Sister Agnes, but they all agreed that she treated me differently. The general consensus was that, for some unknown reason, she seemed to single me out and went out of her way to make my life miserable. She was succeeding.

By now, we were allowed to spend Christmas with our families. Since everyone was leaving the next day to be with relatives, all thirteen of us Sisters ate dinner together on Christmas Eve. I told several of my close friends that I'd be leaving right after dinner, so when my mother arrived at 7 p.m., I slipped quietly away without saying any goodbyes. I had only a single suitcase, having taken my few belongings to the convent section at Emmanuel College the week before. That's where I was going to live while enrolled in Wheelock College for the second semester.

This was my first Christmas home in Beverly Farms in 21 years.

The day after Christmas I drove alone to the Trappist Monastery in Spencer for a three-day retreat, using that time to reflect on the previous five months. The Blessed Sacrament Convent could have been named Purgatory's Gate, as far as I was concerned, because Sister Agnes had made it a living hell for me. I was grateful it was behind me and knew I needed to forget it and think positively about the future. There were new ventures to meet and new obstacles to overcome while I finished at Wheelock College. Once again, hope was on the horizon.

The Sisters of Notre Dame were going through some rough times in the early 1970s. The Massachusetts province was divided into three groups: A, B and C. The A Group was conservatives; B Group was liberals; and C Group was "middle-of-the-roaders." Two communities existed within Emmanuel College — the A and B groups. Because of a lack of space in the B Group, which was liberal, I was assigned to the conservative A Group. I was well received; they welcomed me with open arms and were truly caring, despite knowing nothing about my recent conflicts, my background, or me. All they knew was that I was there because I needed space while attending Wheelock College.

Once again, I was operating under a systematic routine: up at 8 a.m., pick up breakfast in the refectory, attend classes at Wheelock until 4 p.m., evening classes twice during the week, Mass at 5 p.m., dinner, and study before going to bed.

The Reverend Mother in Rome passed down an edict that the province would function as two groups: A and B. I remained in Group A after the proclamation was made. My anxieties began to return. Part of it, I suspect, was the psychological implications of being lumped into a category geared toward maintaining the status quo. I always thought of myself as being a progressive personality and was beginning to feel a desire to contribute to something more worthwhile than my own education. I yearned again for the feeling of helping to make a difference.

When a job as reading specialist in the Portsmouth public school system was offered to me, I thought long and hard about it. I really wanted to go back to New Hampshire. I felt that St. Julie's spirit was destined to live on in that state, and I wanted to be a part of seeing that it did. Besides, the early Sisters had struggled so doggedly to gain acceptance that I felt an obligation to them to continue the tradition. I went to the Provincial, Sister Helen, in March to seek her permission to accept the offer. When she granted it, I pushed the envelope a bit further.

"Thank you, Sister. Would it be possible for me to also gain permission to live alone while there?"

She thought for a moment, and then refused me by saying, "It's not considered community living to live by oneself."

She wanted me to live with another religious order nearby.

"Sister, please," I argued, "there are Sisters living in secular dorms all across the country now who are not living in religious communities. How can you argue that it's against the rules, when it's accepted in other places?"

"Why do you want to live alone?" she consistently wanted to know.

"Because I need a change from community living. I'm tired of cohabiting with others. For the past twenty years or more I've been living in the same space with someone else and I just need to spend some time alone."

"You'll have to come up with a better reason than that," she said, "before you get my approval."

I respected Sister Helen. We'd entered the order the same day, although she was a year or two older. I didn't know it at the time, but the reason she wanted me to live with someone else was because St. Michael's was closing. So many were leaving the order that there simply weren't enough left to staff the school. Sister Helen's insistence that I live communally was based, I think, on a sense that I, too, might be ready to leave; she wanted to prevent that and have me continue the religious life. That, I believe, was her only motive. We always remained on friendly terms, but I was becoming frustrated. I knew that I'd finish my M.A. program in May and that assignments would be finalized for the next school year. Regardless of where I went or what I did, one thing I was sure of: I needed to live alone. I needed space.

I decided to end the debate with Sister Helen and made arrangements to meet with the Provincial of the B province. I discussed my situation with her and expressed my needs. She seemed to understand.

"I'll tell you what we can do," she said. "I'll take you into our province and will bring up your request when I speak at the general meeting next week."

"I appreciate that, Sister. Thank you."

With my good friend, Sister Jon, I worked out a simple plan for starting readiness classes in five Notre Dame schools in Massachusetts, and presented it at the general meeting. It was rejected. And so was permission for me to live alone. That was it. I was at the end of my rope.

Down deep in my heart, I believed that Christianity could be experienced and promoted outside the classroom and outside Notre Dame. I spent most of the next night in the chapel at Emmanuel College, contemplating my future. I prayed long and more soulfully than I had in years for some sort of Divine Guidance to pull me out of the quagmire in which I found myself. A peaceful resolution came over me around 2 a.m. My decision had been made. I would leave Notre Dame after twenty-one years. I had reached the end of that road and it was time to turn off onto another highway. At first, I was reluctant to accept my decision, because I had been very happy with the Sisterhood, for the most part But the next morning, I found myself calling Father Liam to tell him of my decision.

"You can't do that," he cajoled, "the church needs dedicated Sisters like you."

"It's too late," I answered. "My decision is made. It's time I get on with my life."

He tried to persuade me to try another province, but I wasn't interested. Any talk about finding alternative solutions to staying in the order was by this time falling on deaf ears. I had made up my mind.

The next day I called to see Sister Helen. We met for lunch at Simone's in Cambridge. I was taken aback a bit at her calm reaction when I told her of my choice. It was almost as though she expected it.

"I distinctly got the impression that you needed your freedom," she said. "That's why I persistently hounded you to tell me why you wanted to live alone. I was trying to get you to admit it to yourself. I suspect that you're trying to fill a gap you missed from your youth."

"What do you mean?"

"You came to the order straight from high school at — what? Seventeen? You went directly from family life into the convent without ever knowing what it was like to live single and on your own. I waited a couple of years before entering Notre Dame, so I was able to fill that gap. You never had the chance. Believe me, I understand."

"Then am I to infer that I will leave with your blessing?"

"Of course, Sister. We all have to determine what path we must follow to fulfill our destinies. It is not for me to judge what course God mapped out for you. That's between you and Him. You only have my prayers and well wishes to take from me."

"That is comforting to know, Sister. Thank you."

"How do you plan to announce your departure?"

"I'm glad you asked. I would prefer that no one know until after I have left. I will write a letter to the hundred particular Sisters who I want to let know personally. The rest can find out through word of mouth after the fact."

"Okay," she consented, "but allow me one request."

"What's that?"

"Inform your coordinator, Sister Charlotte, in person as soon as possible."

"I will," I hesitantly agreed.

The meeting was ten times more relaxed than I had imagined it would be. I left at peace with myself and with my decision. Somehow, hope was indeed springing eternal and I knew that I was making the right choice. Bright, new adventures awaited me just beyond the horizon. Sad as I was to leave behind something that had been such a large part of my life for so long, my spirit was rejuvenated at the prospect of what lie ahead.

It was time to find out how right Saint Paul was.

Leaving the Sisterhood; Marriage

Peg and Coleman Hogan were good friends from Exeter. They were a highly family-oriented couple. In fact, five of their eleven children had been in my classroom in New Hampshire. When they received word that I was leaving the order, their immediate concern was about my financial well-being. Colie offered me a secretarial job for the summer. He was the chief executive officer of a large company and wanted to help out, at least until my new job started in the fall.

My old friend, Sister Theresé from St. Mary's Cambridge, telephoned me at Emmanuel in mid-May.

"Is it true? Are you leaving the convent?"

I was so stunned by her blunt inquiry that I couldn't give her an honest answer.

"Look," she said, "I'm flying to New York tonight. When I return in two days, I'll come right over to Emmanuel so we can talk."

When I hung up the phone, I couldn't help wondering, "Who has betrayed my confidence?"

Two hours later, Sister Eileen telephoned to say she heard I was leaving. This was exactly what I wanted to prevent from happening. Who was leaving and who did what to whom was the kind of gossip that floated about on recreation nights. I did not want news of my departure to happen that way.

Aunt Eliza bought me an old car for graduation from Wheelock, letting me have it ahead of time so I could begin transporting my belongings home. I was hoping that Sisters Therese and Eileen were the only ones who knew I was leaving. I was pretty sure that none of the local Sisters were aware; otherwise it would be the hottest scuttlebutt circulating around the convent. At any rate, I did not want anyone else to know. It was May 16 and I went through my regular routine of classes, Mass, and dining with the Sisters. I had an evening class and returned about 10, whereupon I loaded my belongings into the car. I was careful to avoid detection by slipping in and out of the corridor as the other Sisters were coming and going to chapel. I waited until midnight to attend chapel when no one else was there, and stayed until about 2:30.

The hundred letters I had prepared announcing my departure were sealed and stamped. I waited in my room until after the early morning hustling quieted down and the long corridors became still and empty. Shortly after 7 a.m., I was able to slip unnoticed out the back door, sneak into my car, mail the letters at the end of the driveway, and secretly steal away into the early morning mist.

Some things are more frightening to an adult than a Halloween mask is to an impressionable child. Facing the unknown is one of them. This foray into unchartered waters may have been worse than that childhood trauma I had experienced.

A strange sensation overcame me. After twenty-one years of total servitude and obedient behavior, I was beginning to feel as though my entire body and soul were being released. It was an unsettling feeling. I didn't realize it at this point, but it was ironic that the length of time I had spent obligated to the convent was almost the same amount of time St. Julie spent constricted by her paralysis. We were both bound by outside forces and emerged dedicated to the same goals, ultimately to serve God.

I needed to go to Mass. I stopped at the shopping mall that housed the Carmelite Chapel in Peabody. The doors were locked until 8:30. That exacerbated my fears. I felt as though the Lord Himself were rejecting me. Filled with apprehension, I wandered into a nearby pancake restaurant and ordered the only thing on the menu that the fifty cents in my pocket would buy — a cup of coffee and a piece of toast.

When I went back to attend Mass at 8:30, I fell apart. I sobbed my heart out. I don't know if I was feeling sorry for myself, if it was loneliness, if I was reacting to being rejected again, or if I was just plain weary. But once the tears flowed and I got it out of my system, I was able to continue my migration home to Beverly Farms.

Mum was waiting for me with Aunt Eliza and Aunt Ann. Nell wasn't there. Almost immediately, Mum made it known that she was not happy about my leaving the convent.

I returned to Boston later that afternoon to prepare preparations for school. I still had to complete my masters. I went to stay in the North End with Ann McCarthy, an old high school friend, who was working in a bank in Boston, and slept on her couch for two weeks.

I called home three days later.

"You need to get in touch with your Provincial and Sister Theresé," Mum spouted at me. "They've been looking everywhere for you and are worried about you."

I'd forgotten about Sister Theresé. Returning from New York on the 17th, she came directly to Emmanuel College that morning, as she had said she would. Unable to find me in my room or on campus, she contacted Sister Anna across the hall from my room.

"She's probably at Wheelock," Sister Anna told her, "as she has a different schedule."

It wasn't unusual for Sisters not to see one another for days, sometimes weeks, at a time. The college was quite large, so they hadn't even missed me.

After two days with no word from or about me, Sister Theresé summoned the Provincial, and the two went to my mother's house. They carried my dowry check of $500. This money, which we were required to bring when entering the convent was to be used as start-up capital if we ever left the order. Mum told them that I was in Boston, but she didn't know exactly where.

I called the Provincial and explained to her why I had left so unexpectedly. I also met with Sister Theresé and laid out the whole story in detail.

I graduated from Wheelock on May 30 and left the Notre Dame order on May 31. The Hogans sponsored a graduation party, which Mum and I attended. After the celebration, I realized that I needed to start looking for a place to live. I was about to begin the job that Colie had arranged for me and needed a roof over my head for the summer.

I stayed at the University of New Hampshire for four weeks. One of the Sisters from another order had a fellowship there, and let me use her room while she was in New Jersey on vacation. It was a difficult adjustment. I was accustomed to having my needs provided for me. Now, I had to fend for myself.

Colie gave me $500 to get started. To a nun, accustomed to having no more than $15 or $20 at a time (in later years), that was a small fortune. There was so much to learn and so much to keep track of. A thirty-eight-year-old opening a checking account is like a four-year-old trying to learn how to drive a tractor-trailer. I must have been a sight to behold at Rich's Department Store checkout counter, trying to figure out how to write my first check for $16.

Father Liam, who was nearby, again came to my aid. He helped me find an apartment in Seabrook, thirty-five minutes from where I worked and only twenty minutes from Portsmouth, where I would start my new public mission as the reading director in the fall.

Dad had a friend who owned a furniture store in Peabody. I bought a living room set and bedroom set for $1,000, which he allowed me to charge. I was making only $100 a week, but my aunt Ann helped out by paying my rent in Seabrook for July and August. Father Liam brought spaghetti for dinner the night I moved in, July 1. There was neither a table nor any dishes, so we shoveled pasta down our throats with a snow scraper from my car. Those are the kind of moments you never forget.

I received a stark education on the ways of the world about midway through the summer. My car died. Fortunately, Colie was right there and helped me finance my first new car. Not much later, my apartment was burglarized. Was God punishing me for leaving? That's what I thought was happening. I didn't realize it at the time, but I was getting to know what lay people meant by the "ups and downs" of life. God didn't have anything to do with it, except, of course, making us human. It was just part of being human.

Dad had been in really poor health in recent months. He was in and out of the hospital during the whole time I was making this transition.

As I finished my summer job and began my challenging new task as a reading specialist in Portsmouth the day after Labor Day, I reflected on this most remarkable year. It was filled with excitement and unexpected twists and turns, but overall, the year 1972 was a major turning point in my life. I left the convent, received a master's degree, acquired an apartment, finished a part-time summer job, and began full-time employment in civilian life — and the year wasn't over yet.

Everyone in Portsmouth was warm and receptive and fascinated that I had spent more than twenty years as a nun. They constantly probed me about my past, wanting to know what it was like and how I could stand such a lifestyle for so long. The one person who somewhat understood what I'd been through was the man who had hired me in the first place — Jim Cusick, the school superintendent. He had been a seminarian, so he had at least an inkling of what the experience was like.

The toughest adjustment was trying to make it with very little money. Without family and close friends, I don't know what I would have done. The mechanics of disassociating from a tight structure like the convent, which provides for all its members' mundane needs, requires the departing person to learn self-reliance — and that was my biggest challenge. But I loved living alone and being free. The sense of independence was what I needed. I suppose that it could have happened in the convent, because changes that encouragted indepenedence within the church were occurring rapidly in the '70s, but it hadn't happened for me. No one seemed to hear my pleas and I never got the sense that I would experience freedom as long as I wore the habit. I guess the Lord just had other plans for me at this stage.

Father Liam and I became closer than ever. He helped me to adjust to the outer world. We got together on a weekly basis to discuss life, changes, spirituality and love. However, he was more than a counselor; he was a friend and my confidant, But even that was changing. The church and religious life was important to both of us. He was instrumental in helping me deal with my dilemma of preferring not to leave Notre Dame but feeling compelled to. We prayed together and made spiritual pacts weekly. He guided me through the insecurities I faced while trying to make it on my own.

We started seeing each other more often. It wasn't long before, I think, we both realized that our friendship was taking an evolutionary turn. It was becoming a relationship.

One night he asked if he could visit with me privately. We talked for hours, mostly about religious life. Suddenly, out of the blue, he said, "I love you."

I was flabbergasted and didn't know how to respond. He continued talking to me, but at that point I was so numb that I didn't hear a word he said — at least for a few minutes. He gently grasped my hand, and looked directly into my eyes.

"May I kiss you?" he asked.

"Yes."

That was the beginning of the relationship. Although it wasn't easy for either of us, it was always on solid ground, because it was based on respect, spirituality and admiration.

His six-year tenure at the monastery was almost up and he had to figure out what the next step in his life would be. He decided to return to school for his doctorate and pursue an avenue that would involve dealing with the aged. He applied to the Ph.D. programs at both Syracuse University and Boston College. When he was accepted at both, he based his decision on our relationship. Knowing that the distance between us that Syracuse would create might have adversely effected the relationship, he opted to enter the psychology department at Boston College. He moved to Boston in September at the same time that I started my new job in Portsmouth.

As the school year elapsed, our relationship grew deeper and stronger. I still hadn't fallen in love, but I cherished our comforting and loving bond.

I wish that my Dad could have gotten to know him, but Dad took very sick at Christmas and never recovered. At my request, Father Liam brought him Holy Communion during his final days, but Dad was never aware of the priest who was comforting him. He died January 9, 1973.

We had carried our relationship about as far as it could go without Father Liam leaving the priesthood. Since I wasn't going back to the convent, he either had to abandon the clergy or we had to break off the relationship. There could be no middle ground.

Father Liam and I shared the secret of our romance with our friends Peg and Colie, who were staunch Catholics. They remained completely supportive during the ensuing stormy months. I was now sharing Father Liam's affection equally. We were in love.

It was not a peaceful trail we faced. In fact, it became downright tumultuous at times. Father Liam had to tell his Superiors that he wanted to leave the priesthood to marry. This was agonizing for him. What made it so difficult was that he had two strong loves in his life and was being forced to give one of them up. It was torturous having to make such a life-altering decision. He desperately wanted to continue to be a priest. If only he could be a married priest — but the church did not permit it. I've always felt the law prohibiting priests from marrying was archaic and should have been revoked. After all, who would be better equipped to understand marital crises — a married priest or a celibate one? Anyway, Liam struggled with his Superiors, who fought to break up the relationship and keep him in the priesthood.

At one point, he told his family, and they were, for the most part, understanding, although his mother was openly disappointed that he considered leaving the priesthood and his brother couldn't understand why he would want to get married when he "had it so easy." Even so, Liam finally came to a conclusion.

He wrote to the Vatican requesting a release from his vows. The canon lawyer told him his request must be accompanied by either of two reasons: He couldn't live a celibate life or he was mentally ill — neither of which was true. He opted instead to honestly state that he had fallen in love with a woman and wished to marry her. Rome denied his request.

We went ahead with our wedding plans. Never completely at peace with his decision, he reluctantly gave up the priesthood, but continued to live in Boston.

We were married in May 1974 in a little chapel in a small New Hampshire town. With our families and close friends present, the Hogans had a lovely catered wedding reception in their home after the ceremony.

We honeymooned in Washington, D.C. We had dinner in the Kennedy Center our first night there and took a cab back to our hotel.

"Ride by the Washington Monument," Liam told the cab driver, "as the lady has never seen Washington."

I leaned over and said, "That lady is now your wife."

It was hard to believe we were husband and wife. What started as a platonic friendship turned into matrimony.

Liam continued his studies, internship and thesis writing for the next two years. He took a part time job at Lowell University and one at Northern Essex College, teaching gerontology. During the next two years he received his license as a psychologist in both New Hampshire and Massachusetts, and set out on a meaningful ministry administering to, and helping others respond to, the aged.

I became department head of the reading program in Portsmouth. That was quite a departure from what I was accustomed to. After dealing with first-graders my whole life, interrelating with teachers and specialists was a radical change. I never regretted one minute of my life in Notre Dame. It made me a better person and provided opportunities that I never would have had otherwise.

It has always been apparent to me that God is running our lives. He allowed Liam and me to meet while we were helping others, and made it possible for us to continue being together and helping others when we left our respective orders. We were never any less devoted or less spiritual because of it. If anything, our devotion, love and commitment to God grew stronger. I think that if more people would simply respond to His invitation, there would be more peace on this planet and more joy in our souls. I knew I would always be a daughter of Saint Julie.

"How good is the good God."

Right now He seemed exceptionally good to me. I couldn't ask for more happiness.

Our marriage lasted fourteen years. I was the breadwinner for the first three years. Liam became a psychologist. When we bought our first home, we added an extension for Liam's practice. He was a kind, concerned person who always made himself available for his clients. Eventually, we were also able to buy a small place on the lake that we used for weekend getaways.

After eleven years supervising the reading program, I had grown tired of administration and considered retiring from education entirely. Liam talked me out of retiring, so I put my feelers out to consider a change. The assistant superintendent of schools, Suzanne, was a good friend. She told me about a pending opening for a principal in an elementary school and suggested it would be a perfect position for me. The school was in a middle class neighborhood that was experiencing some difficult situations between the teachers and parents. It was a challenge that appealed to me, and I spent the next five years as an elementary school principal.

In his heart, Liam never left the priesthood. He threw himself into his work because it was so similar to the work he had done as a priest — counseling others. From the very beginning of our life together as man and wife, he taught, came home late from work, made counseling appointments after hours and, in effect, gave himself over to everyone who demanded his time — except me, for whom he never seemed to have time. That left me feeling that our marriage may have been a mistake and, as time went on, that it was falling apart before it even had gotten started. I kept encouraging him to go to counseling, but he wouldn't. He suggested we get involved with CORPUS, an organization dedicated to getting the church to accept married priests. There was also a group pushing to allow women to become priests. I was supportive of both movements, but felt the first step should be to concentrate on getting married priests accepted. After all, they already had the theological training. Once that obstacle was overcome, then it would be easier to work on getting the church to accept women in this traditionally male position.

Perhaps I misunderstood what Liam was going through. I thought he felt conflict over leaving the priesthood to marry me and I began to feel that he needed to be back in the priesthood, although he was doing priestly things. The truth was that he never felt fulfilled with what he was doing and debated with himself each day if he should continue teaching. He never had any misgivings about our marriage, but he also never gave up hoping for a married priesthood in his lifetime.

The anxiety he felt over his work continued throughout our married life. The turning point came in the last year, when Liam began praying for guidance. He prayed to St. Teresa, the Little Flower, for a sign. He was searching for an answer. Strangely enough, I think I was the one who received the sign, which was his turning to St. Teresa indicated that his fulfillment could only come through the church.

I was tired of my job and tired of the frustration surrounding the priesthood dilemma. I knew that the situation would never change and that the priesthood was Liam's first love. It was simply too painful for both of us. I decided to call it quits.

When I told him it wasn't going to work out, he was devastated. I was on pretty shaky ground myself, but there was no other solution. Since I was the one wanting to terminate the marriage, I was the one who had to leave. We separated and I found an apartment in Exeter.

Several years earlier, our friend Peg had died of a sudden heart attack. Liam and I had spent long hours consoling and counseling Colie on the loss of his wife. He and Peg had always been so close that Colie found it hard to cope with the news a few years later of his best friends' imminent divorce. But he never gave up on either one of us. He was sympathetic to both of us and became quite fatherly in the way he continually reached out to me.

I had our marriage annulled, and Liam soon returned to the priesthood, where he belonged. Divorce was a disconcerting process for me. I had to seek out distractions to overcome the desolation I felt, in addition to getting counseling to help me work through my separation and get my life back together. I signed up with a modeling agency and took a course in modeling. Every Monday evening for six months, I traveled to Boston to learn how to become a model.

As time wore on, my relationship with Colie went through a metamorphosis. His fatherly demeanor toward me gradually changed to affection, and eventually our relationship became romantic. A year later, we were married in the parish church.

As a testimonial of their support, Colie's children all attended our wedding — all, that is, but the son he lost in Vietnam. His oldest son, Paul, served as best man. This meant a lot to me. It was a sign that not only did his ten children support him, but that they accepted me as their stepmother after losing their mother just three years earlier.

Colie had retired from his position as CEO of his company, and he encouraged me to take early retirement from my principal's job so we could spend our winters in Florida. I never would have been able to make these trips if it hadn't been for the willingness of my cousin Bill and his wife Carol to step in and take care of Mum while we were away. The biggest problem I had with this arrangement was that I missed my teachers and students, not to mention my family. Being so far away from them in the Sunshine State left a void that I couldn't seem to fill. Colie, as always, was remarkably understanding. During our second winter in Florida, we sold our condo in Massachusetts and moved back to Exeter for the summer. That made it easier for me to keep in touch with everyone.

A generous and loving father, Colie was devoted to educating his eleven children. I had known this about him for many years, but was just beginning to discover the depth of his compassion and concern. Reaching out to the less-fortunate was part of his nature. He was willing to open his heart and his checkbook, whenever he deemed it worthy, to help the needy. He even went so far as to establish scholarships in the colleges and universities from which his children graduated. As I learned just how kind and spiritual he was, I realized that he was God's gift to me.

I have always felt special in God's eyes. I believe that Colie was a reward from God for responding to His call fifty years ago. God's gift was to let another loving man in my life.

My mother died March 13, 1994, at age 94. She had been highly considerate of others throughout her life, and extremely generous for a woman of modest means. I miss her sense of humor. She was still working and driving until the time she died, calling sixty-five ailing people who lived alone and inspiring them to continue living by saying that there was no room for them up above. If she didn't get a laugh, she would at least get a smile. What a vivacious woman! She had a lot of wonderful qualities. I just wish that somewhere along the line she could have learned to reach out and hug me — just once.

Shortly after moving into a new condo in Florida, Colie and I realized that with such a large family, including nineteen grandchildren, we needed a house. During the next few years, we built a home in Florida and, cutting our ties with New Hampshire, became permanent residents of the state known for its citrus, palm trees and beaches.

I enjoyed the modeling that kept me busy, but it didn't fulfill me in the way I needed. Something was missing. I lacked the feeling of being productive. I found that volunteering at JFK Medical Center in Atlantis soon filled that void. After ten years as a volunteer, it was as if St. Julie's spirit once again had grabbed hold of me. The many hours I spent in community service, including membership on several boards — combined with being a step mom and nanny, was enough to keep me from getting bored.

Life is absolutely beautiful for me. I never gave up hope, so I guess St. Paul was completely and utterly correct — faith, hope and love are our greatest aspirations. I found all three and they, in turn, comforted me. By devoting so much of my life to a religious existence, I have had an enriched life — and my mission continues. That mission is to carry out St. Julie's mission of giving and educating those in need.

You see her slogan — "How good is the good God" — is not a question. It's a statement.